The Romance of the Middle Ages

Nicholas Perkins *and* Alison Wiggins

First published in 2012 by the Bodleian Library
Broad Street
Oxford OX1 3BG

www.bodleianbookshop.co.uk

ISBN: 978 1 85124 295 5

Designed by Dot Little
Body type set in 12/16 Adobe Jenson
Printed and bound by Great Wall Printing, China onto 157 gsm Co Ching matte art

British Library Catalogue in Publishing Data
A CIP record of this publication is available from the British Library

Contents

[...]ien telamoie manoit li ozap furent nue
Quant il vint pres de lost encontre sont ale
Tantost tuit li meillor qui li furent priue
Quant vinrent pres de lui en haut sont estrie
Sire bien viengnies vous & quaues achate
Dites de vos noueles coment aues ouure
Alixand' respont molt ai bien escoute
Que porus ma ledi laidengie & blasme
Et chaitif & frarin ma moi oiant clame
Alixand' demande quels est de quel ae
Je li dis que viex ert maint ior auoit passe
Onques ne fait si chaut ne yuer ne este
Les iex a chacieus tous sont esborbele
Molt est fel & entulles nul nen puet auoir gre
Tout le mont vuet auoir desous sa poeste
Et il me respondi cortois es par uerte
Quant tu de tout son estre ne mas noient cele
De ce le tieng ie molt a viellart radote
Que il cuide conquerre si vilment mon regne
Ja ainchois ne verra .i. mois entier passe
Que il aura le chief desus le bu seure
Quant il ot asses dit & ioi tout escoute
Si pris congie de lui parfont li encline
Amis dist il a moi tien ce brief seelle
Sel me porte alixand' le viellart redote
Et ie li respondi volentiers & de gre
Ves ci le seel doz que ien ai aporte
Chenetiax cire & vin que il ma achate
Quant si home louent grant ioie en ont mene
Grant gap en ont entreus & molt en ont ioue
De poron le roi dynde que il auoit gabe
Entreus sen vont riant dessi quau mestre tref
La descent alixand' au pie li sont ale
Et duc & conte & prince qui molt lont honore
Le iument a fait rendre la dont lot enprunte
Au poure hom cui el fu a bon loier donne
Le vin les chanetiax a primes destrousse
Nul hom ne vit trossel tant fort desbarete
Li un tire lautre boute le sac ont destire
Asses se sont illuec detrait & detire
Veillies moi de mon vin que iai ci aporte
Si le beuons ensamble car il na riens couste
Si mengies ouec moi trestuit par amiste
Ce dient li baron que molt a bien parle
Dont vint li vins auant con auoit trestorne
En tent se sont assis & illuec sont digne
Plus que ne vous diroie a li mengiers couste
Illueques ot beu maint vin & maint herbe
Celui qui laporta nont il mie oublie
Car aincois fu beus con ait dautre gouste
Li rois se fait molt lies quant tel ioie ont mene

Molt se rit alixandres
ains que li bries desplit
Et quant lot desploie
et lescripture uit
Donques se gaba plus
.iiij. tans sen rist
Et a dit a ses homes entendes .i. petit
Porus molt me manece & me tient en despit
Mes oreilles oiant ma hui grant honte dit
Or sai bien son corage par bouce & par escrit
Que sil me pooit prendre quil meust desfit
Il me tolroit [...] teste ia non mendroit respit

ACKNOWLEDGEMENTS

The authors would like to thank the many individuals and institutions whose help has made this book possible, especially the owners or curators of books and other objects who have discussed them with us and allowed them to be illustrated here. At the Bodleian Library and Bodleian Library Publishing we are especially grateful to Samuel Fanous, Andrew Honey, Martin Kauffmann, Richard Ovenden, Dot Little, Janet Phillips, Deborah Susman and Madeline Slaven.

Note on translations and glosses

We have provided translations for texts that we quote from other languages, and for some early English texts. These follow the quoted text, and are placed in brackets. For early English texts that are readable except for some less familiar vocabulary, we have provided glosses (in italics) for individial words or phrases.

Foreword

Libraries should be places of wonder and pleasure, alongside the hard graft of scholarship. It is fitting, then, that the Bodleian Library's exhibition *The Romance of the Middle Ages*, and this accompanying book, celebrate medieval romance, a genre of storytelling painted with glittering colours, heroic gestures and miraculous reversals of fortune. The Bodleian houses one of the richest collections of manuscripts and early printed books containing medieval English romances and related texts. They range from the enormous Vernon Manuscript (MS Eng. poet. a. 1) and the sumptuously illuminated Alexander romances in MS Bodl. 264, to the personal anthology of a fifteenth-century scribe named Rate (MS Ashmole 61) and small fragments stuck with sellotape into an album by the enthusiast Colonel W.E. Moss in the 1920s (MS Eng. poet. d. 208). Such unique survivals help to tell the story of romance itself, emerging as a form of vernacular composition soon after the Norman Conquest, flourishing as a dominant branch of secular narrative in the later Middle Ages, and lying at the root of many kinds of later drama, poetry and prose fiction.

Writers such as Chaucer, Shakespeare, Spenser, Ariosto and Cervantes were all drawn to romance as a source of imaginative energy. *The Romance of the Middle Ages* demonstrates how far romance permeates medieval and later imaginations, not only through these now famous authors, but through anonymous tales, visual media, popular poetry and word of mouth. The Bodleian collections are of huge importance in recording how such stories about public histories and secret desires have come to be told. By preserving the weighty compilation and the ephemeral scrap of paper, the Bodleian has played its own vital role in the understanding of romance. It has also been a place of inspiration for those captivated by the Middle Ages as a time of romance and wonder. From the young William Morris and Edward Burne-Jones inspired by the Bodleian's medieval collections as students, to providing a working base for J.R.R. Tolkien and C.S. Lewis, the Library has nourished both scholarly and imaginative engagement with the medieval. It can even be glimpsed by a new generation as one part of the fictional setting for the library at Hogwarts in the film adaptations of *Harry Potter*, the phenomenal success of which is part of our continuing fascination with romance stories of magic, quest and adventure. The Bodleian continues to engage with these traditions and acquire new caches of material such as the archive of Alan Garner, author of *The Weirdstone of Brisingamen*, whose native Cheshire is also the linguistic origin of one of the greatest medieval romances, *Sir Gawain and the Green Knight*.

The Romance of the Middle Ages has seen a number of exciting collaborations. We are very grateful to all the institutions and individuals who have lent material to the exhibition: the Ashmolean Museum; the British Library; the British Museum; Jesus College, Oxford; North East Lincolnshire Archives; the Victoria and Albert Museum; Mr Terry Jones; and Mr Philip Pullman. We are also grateful to the excellent work of the Exhibitions Team at the Bodleian, led by Madeline Slaven, and to the curatorial staff of the Department of Western Manuscripts, especially Dr Martin Kauffmann, Curator of Medieval Manuscripts, and to Dr Samuel Fanous and the staff of Bodleian Library Publishing. The Bodleian's exhibitions and associated publications are now routinely developed in conjunction with academic research projects, and we have enormously enjoyed working with the lead curator, Dr Nicholas Perkins of the English Faculty and St Hugh's College, and his collaborator Dr Alison Wiggins of the University of Glasgow. This exhibition and book once again demonstrate that Oxford's renowned collections and its research activities are a compelling combination.

Sarah E. Thomas
Bodley's Librarian and Head of Bodleian Libraries

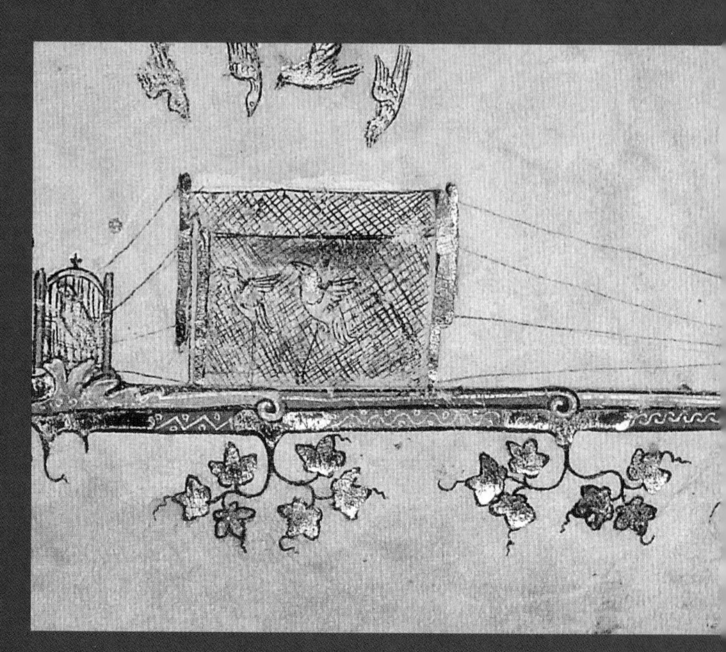

CHAPTER 1

Nicholas Perkins

ROMANCE and the MEDIEVAL WORLD

PICTURE THE SCENE. A magnificent dining hall, tables laden with food. Knights and ladies flirting, dancing and playing Christmas games. Costly eastern fabrics, fashioned into the latest styles. On the raised dais sit King Arthur and Queen Guinevere, with the cream of the Round Table, including Sir Gawain, Sir Ywayne and Sir Agravayne. Arthur, the poet tells us, requires 'sum aduenturus þing, an vncouþe tale / Of sum mayne meruayle þat he myȝt trawe, / Of alderes, of armes, Of oþer auenturus' (an adventure story, a strange tale of some great marvel that he'd believe in, of princes, of combat, of other escapades), or to witness a knightly challenge before eating.[1] As if summoned by this Arthurian yearning for adventure, into the hall rides a huge knight, exquisitely dressed, his small waist and powerful mien demanding the admiration of men and women alike. In one hand he holds a threatening axe, in the other a festive holly branch. The courtiers stare in amazement: the knight and his horse are totally green.

This moment of anticipation and surprise is taken from one of the greatest narrative poems in English, *Sir Gawain and the Green Knight*, written in the late fourteenth century in a dialect from north-west England. A fantasy of the mythic British past and yet sharply contemporary in descriptive detail, *Sir Gawain and the Green Knight* embodies many of the elements that make romance such a rewarding genre. Arthur's criteria for entertainment – adventure, novelty, the marvellous, feats of arms and story-telling – are all characteristic of romance, which engages its audiences by teasing or satisfying their desires in narrative form. Such desires can include a taste for the grotesque and miraculous, for love frustrated and consummated, for religious and military conflict, for acts of shocking violence and uncalculating generosity. While indulging in the pleasures of the fictive, however, romances also focus our attention on how individuals act and interact at moments of crisis or decision, and ask an implicit question of their audience: what would *you* do if this happened to you?

Back at Camelot, the *Gawain*-Poet draws us into the circle of awe-struck courtiers gazing at the Green Knight. We too must weigh his challenge: to chop off his head, and in a year's time to face a return blow. His uncanny mingling of deadly earnest and festive game probes the Arthurian court's reputation for chivalric prowess. The only surviving manuscript of *Sir Gawain and the Green Knight* illustrates this episode (fig. 1). At the upper level, Gawain gains Arthur's permission to accept the challenge in the king's stead. In the lower portion, the Green Knight has fetched his severed head as it rolls at the terrified courtiers' feet; the head then speaks, reminding Gawain of his promise to suffer a return blow. The figures on the dais now double as startled onlookers, and the splendidly green horse stares directly at Gawain. The gory head and huge axe dominate the centre of the picture. King Arthur has been upstaged, while Guinevere's green robe accentuates the Green Knight's own colour, though the artist has baulked at painting his face and hair in the 'enker grene' (line 150: vivid green) so minutely

Figure 1. The only surviving manuscript of *Sir Gawain and the Green Knight* contains a number of striking pictures, this one placed just before the romance begins. In the upper level Gawain takes up the Green Knight's challenge, with Arthur, Guinevere and possibly Agravayne at the table. In the lower level, the severed head speaks. London, British Library, MS Cotton Nero A.x, fol. 90v © British Library Board (England, *c.* 1400).

described in the text. In Chapter 4 we shall return to Gawain, this time pinned to his bed by a gorgeous married woman. The drama of this opening scene, however, already provides a number of ways in which to consider how romance inhabited the Middle Ages in Britain.

Hearing no response to his initial challenge, the Green Knight mockingly asks: 'What, is þis Arthures hous ... Þat al þe rous rennes of þurȝ ryalmes so mony?' (lines 309–10: What? Is this really Arthur's court, whose fame runs through so many realms?). In an arena where your reputation can be tantamount to who you are, romance protagonists often have to forge their identity afresh in response to a catastrophic loss of name. This situation generates the characteristic romance scenario of a lone knight seeking adventure (from French *aventure*, implying fate, or chance), as explored in Eric Auerbach's classic study *Mimesis*.[2] However, romance identities stretch beyond young male protagonists, often revolving around family relationships, land and belief: in these stories, identities are realized in relation to others. In the fourteenth-century poem *Sir Eglamour of Artois*, for example, the young hero's lover Cristabell gives birth to their child, and her jealous father casts mother and baby out to sea. After her boy is snatched away by a griffon, she is washed ashore and sheltered by the local ruler (fig. 2). Later, when her now-grown foundling son wants to marry her, she discovers his identity, and averts their incestuous union, because he uses a griffon and child as his heraldic emblem. Finally, Eglamour himself comes to challenge for her hand. Having defeated his son in a tournament, he too is recognized by Cristabell due to his new emblem: a ship with woman and child. In this romance, the strength of family

Her maydens wepte echeone
Her mother in a sowne dyd fall
Right so dyd her frendes all
That woulde her any goode
Good lorde she sayed nowe I youe praye
Lett some preste a gospell saye
For dowte of fendes in the flode
Fare well she sayd my maydens fre
Grete well my lorde whan youe hym see
They wepte as they were woode

Leaue we nowe of Syr Eglamoure
And speke we more of that ladye floure
That vnknowen wayes yode
The shippe droue forthe nyght and daye
Vp to a roche the sothe to saye
Where wylde beastes dyd renne
She was full fayne I vnderstande
She wende she had ben in some lande
And vp than gan she wende
No maner of menne founde she there
But foules and beastes that wylde were
That faste fledde from her hande
There came a gryffon that wrought her care
Her yonge chylde a waye he bare
In to a countrey vnknowen
The lady wepte and saide alas
That euer she borne was
My chylde ys taken me from
The kinge of Israell on huntynge wente
He sawe where the foule lente
And towarde hym gan he go
A gryffon the boke sayeth that he hyght
That in Israell dyd he lyght
That wrought that ladye wo
The foule smote hym with hys byll
The Childe cryed and lyked yll
The gryffon lefte hym than
A gentleman to that gan passe
In a mantell of scarlet lapped yt was
And with a ryche pane
The chylde was large of lymme and lythe
A gyrdle of golde yt was bounde withe

bonds is only fully realized once they have been broken and remade through suffering and violence.

Cycles of integration–disintegration–reintegration are at the core of these traditional narratives, or 'symbolic stories', which share many motifs with folktale and ballad. Often they end with marriage, wealth and acclaim, while the disloyal or inconvenient are punished: that is, cultural norms are reinforced and celebrated. But these are rather loose ends, soon unpicked. The imaginative space that romances open can enable dark fantasies of infanticide, incest, betrayal and exile to be explored, and this space feeds the imagination long after the text closes. Thus romance stories spin off from one another, with continuations, adaptations, and the reprise of favourite motifs and heroes such as Gawain. He appears in *The Jeaste of Sir Gawayne* just before *Sir Eglamour of Artois* in Bodleian MS Douce 261, a manuscript dated 1564 and hand-copied from printed romances (see also figs 58 and 59). The *Jeaste*'s Gawain, who fights a series of opponents objecting to his possession of a nameless woman, has something of the franchise-weariness of Roger Moore's later James Bond films: punchlines delivered, enemies dispatched, women bedded, but without much conviction. We should not, however, imagine that this marks a general waning of romance from some pure origin: the Gauvain of early French romances is already an unreliable philanderer, while the chronicle tradition continues to depict him as Arthur's doughty lieutenant. Gawain's 'identity', then, is a palimpsest of different stories told from a wide range of traditions. This variety allows for unpredictable interactions between versions of Gawain, as Thomas Malory found in his attempt to compile many sorts of Arthurian stories into one book.

Figure 2. Numerous pen-and-ink drawings adapted from printed books illustrate this manuscript's romances. Here, in *Sir Eglamour of Artois*, Cristabell's child is snatched away by a griffon. The remembrance of this moment will be a crucial turning point later in the story. Oxford, Bodleian Library, MS Douce 261, fols 39v–40r (England, dated 1564).

Writing a publisher's preface to Malory's *Le Morte Darthur* in 1485, William Caxton acknowledges the confusing multiplicity of the work, and by extension of romance as a whole: 'For herein may be seen noble chyvalrye, curtosye, humanyté, frendlynesse, hardynesse, love, frendshype, cowardyse, murder, hate, vertue, and synne. Doo after the good and leve the evyle, and it shal brynge you to good fame and renommee [renown].'[3]

Every literary genre is a thing of shreds and patches, and romance is constantly overlapping, mingling with and reforming the stories that medieval writers called *tale, lay, storie, fable, song, spel, geste, romaunce*. As Chapter 3 suggests, the surviving books containing romances give us valuable evidence about how medieval readers understood and developed this variety, and allow us to speculate about reasons for copying them with other material – from a desire for improving literature to a fascination with exotic lands. Attempts have been made to categorize romances as 'chivalric', 'popular', 'Arthurian', 'penitential' or 'burlesque'; such attempts raise good questions, but are at best partial. Thinking about genre, then, is more like studying the mix of colours on a palette than biological taxonomy.[4] *Sir Gawain and the Green Knight* begins with a grandiose classical reference to Troy, but then claims an oral tradition: the narrator will tell his 'laye ... as I in toun herd' (lines 30, 31: tale, as I heard it in town) and also calls it 'an outrage awenture of Arthures wonderes' (line 29: an amazing happening from Arthur's marvels). With its feasting, sexual temptation and magic, the poem might seem highly secular, but Gawain's task is to uphold his *trawþe* (truth, loyalty, faith); the story is woven around Christian festivals and symbolism; and in British Library MS Cotton Nero A. x the poem

Figure 3. At this point in *The Canterbury Tales*, Chaucer's alter ego is interrupted by the Host, and turns from the tail-rhyme romance *Sir Thopas* (whose distinctive layout still affects the conversation on this page) to the prose allegory *Melibee*. The illustration reinforces the greater authority accorded to *Melibee*'s weighty theme of curbing violence by reason and counsel. Oxford, Bodleian Library, MS Rawl. poet. 223, fol. 183r (England, mid-fifteenth century).

Chaucer

In Which there be som mirthe or doctryne . Gladly quod I be goddis swete pyne .
I wol you telle a litill thing in prose
That ought to like you as I suppose — } It is a morall tale vertuous
All be it tolde somtyme in sondry wise
Of sondry folk as I shall you devyse . } And thus ye wot that euery Euangelist .
That tellith us the peyne of Jhu crist
Ne saith all thing as his felawes doth } But yet his sentence is all soth .
And alle accorden as in her sentence
All be there in here telling difference . } ffor som of hem more and som lesse .
When thei his pitous passion expresse
I mene of Marc . Mathew . luke . and John } But douteles her sentence is all oon .
Therfor lordinges alle I you beseche
If that you thinke that I varye in my speche } As thus if I telle somwhat more .
Of Proverbes than ye haue herd before
Comprehendid in this litill tretice here } To enforce the effect of my matere .
And thought I nat the same wordes seye
As ye han herd yet to alle you I praye } Blameth nought me for as in my sentence .
Yet shall ye fynde difference
ffor this sentence of this tretice lite } After which this mery tale I write .
And herkeneth what that I shall say
And late me telle my tale I pray .

Here endith the tale of Maister Chaucer .

And here ye shal fynde a moral tale of Melibe and Prudence

Young man callid Melibe .
mighty and riche begat his wif that cal ,, vpon
led was Prudence a doughter which that
callid was Sophie Upon a day befel that he
for his disport he went in to the feldes
him to play his wif and eke his doughter
hath he left withynne his hous of

sits alongside three virtuosic religious poems by the same author, now titled *Pearl, Cleanness* and *Patience.*

Chaucer's *The Canterbury Tales* equally illustrates the fluidity of romance. Several tales take romance forms, from the classically grounded *Knight's Tale* of Palamon and Arcite's rivalrous love for Emily, to the *Squire's Tale* of marvels and exoticism. The Franklin tells a 'Breton lay' – a short form often involving enchantment and transformation – while *The Wife of Bath's Tale* is an Arthurian romance whose protagonist rapes a young woman and is disciplined by the ladies of the court: his punishment is to discover what women most desire. *The Man of Law's Tale* and *The Clerk's Tale* describe women treated cruelly, but whose fortitude issues an immediate ethical challenge to the audience. In addition, Chaucer stages the pilgrims' reaction to these stories, reminding us how audiences are imagined and appealed to in romances. After *The Knight's Tale,*

In all the route nas ther yong ne oold	*group—there was neither*
That he ne seyde it was a noble storie	*a noble (hi)story*
And worthy for to drawen to memorie,	*store in the memory*
And namely the gentils everichon.[5]	*especially the high-ranked folk*

Here we are shown distinctions of young and old, low birth and 'gentil' amidst the praise. But audiences, like genres, are unpredictable, and the hegemony of this version of romance – weighty, aristocratic, highly textual – is immediately undermined by *The Miller's Tale*, with its arse-kissing, hot-poker-thrusting *fabliau* version of the story of a girl with two lovers, set not in classical Thebes but in contemporary Oxford. The romance told by Chaucer's alter ego also receives a powerful reaction. Using the lilting tail-rhyme stanzas often thought quaint by Chaucer's time, *Sir Thopas* is a parodic

Figure 4. Scenes from the 'Foray of Gaza' episode of the *Roman d'Alexandre.* The third level down shows Alexander on the left; on the right some knights debate who should leave the battle to ask him for help. Faces in the roundels provide a scrutinizing audience, and the *bas-de-page* images relieve and perhaps mock the high drama of the main picture. Oxford, Bodleian Library, MS Bodl. 264, fol. 21v (Flanders; illustrations completed 1344).

Cest si comme li home alixandre aleient en feure el ual de iosafaille et coment cil de tyr le desfendirent
et coment emmenidus darrabe ne pot trouuer en s la sue gent ki noncier le uosist a alixandre.

ragbag of romance clichés, of giants and love-longing, its teller appealing to famous heroes such as Horn and Guy of Warwick just as his audience loses interest. The Host interrupts this 'rym dogerel', crying 'Thy drasty [*wretched*] rymyng is nat worth a toord!' (fig. 3).[6] Chaucer's Canterbury romances, jostled between prose treatises, saint's lives, fables and *fabliaux*, give us a particularly lively sense of romance's variety of forms, and an audience's power to judge one tale noble and another execrable.

Part of the pleasure that romance generates is in the evocation of cloud-capped towers and gorgeous palaces, the splendour of tournament and battle, without the many inconveniences of medieval travel and warfare. One magnificently illustrated collection of Alexander romances in the Bodleian Library includes dozens of pictures showing the public glory of Alexander's conquests (MS Bodl. 264; fig. 4). The stories of Alexander and some of the other 'Nine Worthies' were used as gauges for those aspiring to chivalric honour, and seeking precedents for war against eastern peoples. Romance narratives and ideas were cultivated in medieval courts throughout Britain as part of a political landscape, projecting images of power, courtesy and restraint. After the text of *Sir Gawain and the Green Knight*, someone has written 'Hony soyt qui mal pence' (shame to him who thinks ill of it), the motto of the Order of the Garter, founded by Edward III allegedly to save the blushes of a lady whose garter slipped from her leg while dancing. Romances provided fertile grounds for debating and emulating honourable and shameful acts. Courts staged re-enactments of romance scenes and Arthurian tournaments, and noble families fiercely guarded the rights to their heraldic emblems along with their accompanying

Figure 5. This manuscript records heraldic emblems of English noble families. Here, the Earl of Derby's crest includes a child snatched by an eagle. This motif recalls a romance-style story about an ancestor of the Stanley family, who discovered a child in an eagle's nest. The motif is preserved in the name of The Eagle and Child pub in Oxford, a regular meeting place for J.R.R. Tolkien, C.S. Lewis and the other Inklings. Oxford, Bodleian Library, MS Rawlinson B. 39, p. 9 (England, 1561).

narratives of origin (fig. 5). The Norfolk gentleman John Paston III, writing to his mother Margaret in 1468, described a tournament in Bruges for the wedding of Princess Margaret to Charles the Bold, Duke of Burgundy: 'As for the Duke's court, as of lords, ladies, and gentlewomen, knights, squires, and gentlemen, I heard never of none like it save King Arthur's court.' Paston owned a copy of *The Grene Knight* (a version of the well-known Gawain story) as well as works by Chaucer, and his interest in tournaments and chivalry is evidenced in his personal manuscript, the 'Grete Boke', which mingles texts on conduct, knighthood and romance.[7]

Romance's interaction with medieval culture was not confined to the public realm, however, and romance protagonists must frequently escape a stifling or corrupt court. Lovers seek a private space to speak or make love, though in the Middle Ages being alone was a relative concept, hence the many narratives involving prying eyes and gossiping tongues. A set of ivory panels in Oxford's Ashmolean Museum includes scenes of lovers in a garden, a game of backgammon, and a lady armed with a branch, spurring into action against a knight (fig. 6). They once formed a box that may have been a lover's gift. The scenes share motifs with a number of romances, including *Huon of Bordeaux*, which in its sixteenth-century English translation includes a game of chess played for a princess's virtue (she loses deliberately, but the hero refuses to take up his 'winnings'), and a woman posing as a man, before being transformed into one by God so that s/he may marry her/his lover. Other such caskets depict Arthurian romance heroes, or an assault on the castle of love, with its associations of sexual conquest (fig. 7, and see fig. 38). What messages did these caskets give to their

Figure 6. Ivory boxes carved with romance stories and courtship scenes were a popular gift in aristocratic circles. In one panel here, a lady spurs into action against a knight, wielding a flourishing branch in a comic battle of the sexes. Other panels include lovers in a garden; an elopement or kidnap; and a game of backgammon as a figure for love's strategies and conquests. © Ashmolean Museum, University of Oxford, AN2008.27 (Paris, early fourteenth century).

recipients? While their iconography employs recurrent motifs, the personal imaginings that such romance scenes provoked are likely to be highly varied and individual.[8]

A romance, then, could project religious or courtly ideologies, but its very adaptability means that rarely is a story wholly controlled by them. Tellingly, Chrétien de Troyes' influential and engaging French romances, written in the late twelfth century, imagine romance stories emerging in an interlude between Arthur's serious military campaigns.[9] Romance time is not always linear or consistent: it can fold back on itself, or split into fragments, allowing space for unlikely conquests both military and sexual. So in *Sir Eglamour of Artois,* father and son become rivals for one woman's hand; in the Grail romances, knights, beasts and maidens follow interweaving paths through dense narrative forests. Its openness to multiple stories and meanings makes romance liable to criticism as an immoral distraction, and to appropriation for serious or comic ends. One of the earliest English texts to develop romance motifs for a religious purpose is the thirteenth-century treatise for female recluses, *Ancrene Wisse,* which imagines Christ as a lover-knight rescuing a lady besieged in her castle: 'Would not this lady have a base nature if she did not love him after this above all things?'[10] The author harnesses romance's power to provoke female desire, and links Christ's bloody shield – signifying his stretched, crucified body – with the familiar sight of shields hung in churches for remembrance. A version of *Ancrene Wisse* is preserved in the massive compilation now Bodleian MS Eng. poet. a. 1 (the Vernon Manuscript) along with religiously toned romances *The King of Tars* and *Robert of Sicily* (fig. 29). Also included is *Piers Plowman,*

Figure 7. This beautiful casket matches the assault on love's castle on the lid, with the story of Aristotle and Phyllis, the fountain of youth, and Arthurian figures around the sides. The back depicts Gawain fighting a lion; Lancelot crossing a sword-bridge; Gawain on the 'perilous bed' with swords raining down; and ladies who congratulate him after he survives the ordeal. The Gawain episodes derive from Chrétien de Troyes' romance *Perceval.* Victoria and Albert Museum, 146-1866. (Paris, early fourteenth century). Photo © Victoria and Albert Museum, London.

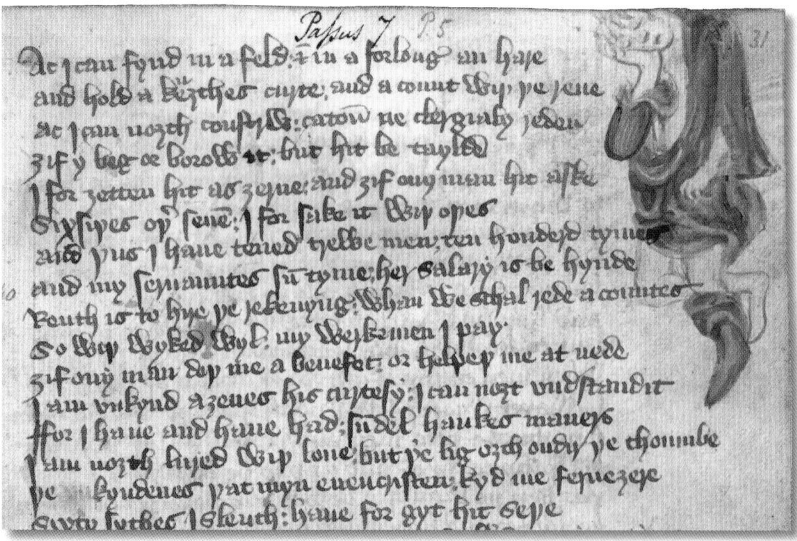

Figure 8 *left.* The confession of Sloth in William Langland's poem *Piers Plowman.* Sloth protests to Repentance that he must sit to confess or he will fall asleep. The artist has portrayed him *déshabillé,* both spiritually and literally dopey; in the text he has 'two slymy eyes'. Oxford, Bodleian Library, MS Douce 104, fol. 31r (Anglo-Irish, early fifteenth century).

Figure 9. This manuscript contains a wealth of inventive and darkly comic marginal illustrations. Oxford, Bodleian Library, MS Bodl. 264 (Flanders; illustrations completed 1344): fol. 76r (an audience watches a knightly puppet show); fol. 81r (a simian dance); fol. 81v (giant hares hunt men); fol. 98v (monks and nuns playing piggyback).

William Langland's great alliterative poem on Christian belief and action. He imagines Christ as a knight come to joust for humanity, his bloody wounds paradoxically proving his victory over Death. Earlier in *Piers Plowman,* however, Sloth confesses that 'I can [*know*] rymes of Robyn Hode and Rendolf erle of Chestre / Ac [*but*] of oure lord ne of oure lady the leste that euere was maked' (fig. 8).[11] Here popular stories and romances of local heroes are a lazy alternative to prayerful devotion. From all sides, romance can be blended, elevated, parodied. While Alexander the Great bestrides the globe, *bas-de-page* pictures in Bodleian MS Bodl. 264 turn the world upside down, with knights as puppets, cavorting monkeys, nuns piggybacking on monks, and little men falling prey to giant hares (fig. 9).

In the hugely popular French poem *The Romance of the Rose,* the tangled allegory of a dreamer seeking to pluck the rose he desires is

pour lur roy
quant se sent desloyes
A grant ioie cheuauchent les puis de ual garni
us larchon de derriere & celui deuant
tuit ·uy· be

Dont iura fors de la tourner
Sus a lassault sans seiourner.
Ce dit amours appertement

Dont larmet tuit communement.
De telz armes come armer deurent.

Du siege du dieu damours.

Armez sont et bien armez feurent.
Sont saillis sus tuit abrivez
Au fort chastel sont arrivez.
Dont ia ne bevent a partir.
Tant que tuit y seront martir.
Ou quilz soient pris ains quilz sen partent.
Leurs batailles en quatre partent.
Tilz qui les sieges faire deurent.
Partent sont et quant partis feurent.
Si sen vont en quatre parties.
Si com leur gent orent parties.
Pour assaillir les quatre portes.
Dont les gardes neurent pas mortes.
Ne malades ne paresseuses.

La facon de faulx semblant et abstinence contrainte

Or vous diray la contenance.
De faulx semblant et dabstinence.
Qui contre malle bouche vindrent.

wrapped around with parodic romance imagery, for example of the God of Love besieging the castle of Jealousy (fig. 10). Here romance, Ovidian irony and religion combine to spawn the bastard God Cupid, directing a military campaign to capture love's prize. John Gower's major English poem *Confessio amantis* (*A Lover's Confession*), written in the late 1380s, combines this ironic treatment of human desire familiar from *The Romance of the Rose* with a host of exemplary stories. Gower's alter ego, Amans (Lover), confesses to every deadly sin, committed in the pursuit of love. His confession is heard not by a Christian priest but by Genius, priest of Venus, whose answering stories combine romance adventure and revelation with an undertow of ethical seriousness that culminates with a book of advice on kingship that Aristotle supposedly gave Alexander (fig. 11). Gower's *Confessio* is an apt place to conclude this introduction to romance's presence in medieval culture: he takes it for granted that romance is the narrative mode that appeals to the broadest range of readers; he places romance stories alongside the classical and biblical as carriers of meaning and debate; and his textual guise as Amans flavours the deeply political messages – about the (ab)use of power and the need for self-scrutiny – that his writing seeks to convey.[12] His poem's crowning narrative is that of Apollonius of Tyre, an originary story for the romance tradition. Apollonius's survival through violent buffetings of fortune, escape from the jealous, incestuous father of his beloved, shipwreck and despair, and the parallel adventures of his wife and daughter, make the tale an ideal medium for Gower's reflection on the need to heal divisions in self and society. Two hundred years later, 'ancient Gower' appears on stage in Wilkins's and Shakespeare's close adaptation of this story, *Pericles, Prince of*

Figure 10. This illustration from *The Romance of the Rose* depicts the God of Love besieging the castle built on the orders of Jealousy to protect the Rose. In the smaller picture, False and Constrained Abstinence, disguised as pilgrims, make their way to the castle. This fine manuscript was made for Louise of Savoy, mother of Francis I of France. Oxford, Bodleian Library, MS Douce 195, fol. 86v (France, late fifteenth century).

Tyre. Gower acts as prologue, embodying the power of old romance stories to reshape themselves for new audiences – a topic to which we shall return throughout this book:

> To sing a song that old was sung,
> From ashes ancient Gower is come,
> Assuming man's infirmities, *taking on*
> To glad your ear and please your eyes.
> It hath been sung at festivals,
> On ember-eves and holy-ales; *fast-day eves*
> And lords and ladies in their lives
> Have read it for restoratives.
> The purchase is to make men glorious, *profit*
> *Et bonum quo antiquius, eo melius.*[13]
> [And if something is good, the older it is the better.]

Figure 11. Early in John Gower's *Confessio amantis*, the poet's alter ego Amans kneels to confess his sins to Genius. This portrait has been attributed to the skilled artist Herman Scheerre, who probably came to London from Cologne. Oxford, Bodleian Library MS Bodl. 294, fol. 9r (England, early fifteenth century).

Was redy þer and sette him doun
To here my confessioun

Confessus Genio si sit medicina salutis
Experiar morbis quos tulit ipsa Venus
Lesa quidem ferro medicantur membra saluti
Raro tamen medicum vulnus amoris habet.

This worþi prest þis holy man
To me spekende þus bigan

D re entrez bels am
D es idunc entrat l
K e a Wikle tal so
V iuir le reuderunt
V ukes anetes neu
A l palais sentunt
V eient Wikle seer a
I uste bels nigun k
L ors se marrit dan
L es chapes sachent
P le tre sun chair des
T ar ne lur eschale
A eshalbes sunt venus
P ces tables sen uin
T ut del ke de mes
K a nul nes acoint
K e g Wikle seit nuo
M es la gent veihut
E hom net nis Wikle
T el lui douat alchne
P uis lad fet fors sa
E pendre al quefust q
S ulunc quod de sun
U int ke des citors fu
L ad veis .h. de set n
E qant il sunt tenuz
T uz les xi. cors ad
H om ad mere al rei
E n il ad nassaluit s
E um il del paleis ad
D e quikil or fet ne
P la feste sen Wiur c
H i ad nul que nen art

CHAPTER 2

Nicholas Perkins

EMPIRES *of* ROMANCE

MANY STORIES grew up surrounding the Norman Conquest of England, from Harold Godwinson's arrow in the eye to Hereward the Wake's resistance movement. One of the most colourful was that at the Battle of Hastings, a member of Duke William's retinue named Taillefer rode before the troops singing of a great battle from French mythic history:

Taillefer, qui mult bien chantout, sor un cheval qui tost alout, devant le duc alout chantant de Karlemaigne e de Rollant, e d'Oliver e des vassals qui morurent en Rencevals.[1]	[Taillefer, who sang very well, rode before the Duke on a swift horse, singing about Charlemagne and Roland, and Oliver and the knights who died at Roncevaux.]

In this version from Robert Wace's *Roman de Rou* (1160s–70s), Taillefer strikes the battle's first blow, and with impetuous *élan* is last seen surrounded by English warriors. Other versions involve a nameless *jongleur* (minstrel) singing or juggling with swords. Wace's long poem about Norman history was probably commissioned by King Henry II. Here, he transfers the religious and heroic aura surrounding Roland and Charlemagne onto William the Conqueror, helping to justify the Norman colonization of England. Wace's previous major work, the *Roman de Brut*, had chronicled British

Figure 12. In a climactic passage from *La Chanson de Roland*, Roland blows his horn to summon help from Charlemagne. The poem's distinctive refrain call 'AOI' punctuates the verses, or *laisses*, on this folio. Oxford, Bodleian Library, MS Digby 23 (part 2), fol. 32r (England, *c.* 1125–1150).

Sire Roll' e uos sire oliuer.
Pur deu uos pri ne uos cuntraliez.
Ja li corners ne nos auereit mester.
Mais ne pur quant si est il aser melz.
Venget li reis si nus purrat uenger.
Ja cil despaigne ne sen deiuent turner liez.
Nostre franceis i descendrunt a pied.
Truuerunt nos e morz e detrenchiez.
Leuerunt nos en bieres sur sumers.
Si nus plurrunt de doel e de pitet.
Enfuerunt en aitres de musters.
Nen mangerunt ne lu ne porc ne chen.
Respunt Roll' sire mult dites bien. AOI.
Roll' ad mis lolifan a sa buche.
Empeint le ben par grant uertut le sunet.
Halt sunt li pui e la uoiz est mult lunge.
Granz .xxx. liwes loirent il respundre.
Karles loit e ses cumpaignes tutes.
Co dit li reis bataille funt nostre hume.
E guenelun li respundit encuntre.
Saltre le desist ia semblast grant mencunge. AOI.
Li quens Roll' par peine e par ahans.
Par grant dulor sunet sun olifan.
Par mi la buche en salt fors li cler sanc.
De sun ceruel le temple en est rumpant.
Del corn quil tient loie en est mult grant.
Karles lentent ki est as porz passant.
Naimes li duc loid si lescultent li franc.

mythic history up to the Saxon invasions, including King Arthur's conquests and fall. Adapting Geoffrey of Monmouth's brilliant Latin pseudo-history *Historia regum Britanniae* (*History of the Kings of Britain*), Wace's *Brut* and its English version by Layamon provided a latticework of events around which stories, songs and romances flourished. Defeat and invasion, with Norman dominance in language and culture, led to an intense scrutiny about origins, status and power in Anglo-Norman Britain. We can see this at work in books written not only in Latin but also in the vernacular – or *romans* in French: a word that comes to designate the romance genre itself.

The earliest surviving copy of *La Chanson de Roland*, a poem now regarded as the French national epic, survives in Bodleian Library, MS Digby 23 (part 2). Folio 32r (fig. 12) describes Roland's fatal call on his horn to summon help against a huge Saracen army, while the traitor Ganelon tricks Charlemagne into delaying his rescue:

> Li quens Rollant, par peine e par ahans,
> Par grant dulor, sunet sun olifan.
> Parmi la buche en salt fors li cler sancs:
> De sun cervel le temple en est rumpant.[2]

> [Count Roland, in pain, in anguish and great sorrow, sounds his horn. Blood gushes clear from his mouth; around his brain the temple is ruptured.]

Many have imagined this poem in a *jongleur*'s repertoire, but the Oxford manuscript points elsewhere. *La Chanson de Roland* was bound with a copy of Plato's *Timaeus* early on, perhaps by the time of a thirteenth-century note recording that Master Henry of Langley bequeathed the *Timaeus* to the Augustinian canons

Figure 13. In the final lines of the Anglo-Norman *Romance of Horn*, the poet Thomas names himself and rounds off with a Latin prayer. His virtuosic monorhymed *laisses* are emphasized by the separation of the first and last letters of each line on the manuscript page. Bodleian Library, MS Douce 132, fol. 22v (England, mid-thirteenth century).

ꝑ fei dist li porter teis nad lempeo k

o re entrez bels amis ia uer cūtreditor
M es ia nule entrat li 7 li son baldement
ke a Wikle tal sons ferūt ia tel p̄let
V unt le tendrūt tut mat entre 7 dolēt
v nkes auetes neu out nl' petir ingenīt
a l palais sē entre uenēt al pauement
v eient Wikle seer al pl' halt mādeīt
j une bele kigūn ki la face resplen
l ors se marist dan h. e cel nuisemen
l es chapes sachent tost q̄ lor trē muscent
ꝑ le ire sē chair des colps li estrumē
c ar ne lur eschalt q̄l p̄t nl' del c̄e nep̄nt
a shalbs sē remis tret sē li biss trechēt
ꝑ ces tables sen unt ṡuir les maleūt
t ut del ke de mes. v. de mestre prernē
k a nul nz atent ke ne seit fet sāglēt
k e p Wikle seit innoet. v. seit de sa gent
m es la gent rei hunlaf cil ūt espuent
e horn uet ūs Wikle. manecant mlt forment
t el lui donat al chief. ke trestut le pfēt
p uis lad fet fors sacher ē ū mattin pullēt
e pendre al q̄refus q̄ lein el gardement
s ulunc q̄d de sunt sun ṡuise lui rent
P uis ke des ēūtors fud la sale voisde
ad reis h. de sei ueit tute sa gēt mādee
e q̄nt il sūt uenuz la feste ꝫ cumēce
t uz les xv. iors ad noblemēt dure
h orn ad mtre al rei ē la chose ꝫ ale
c ū il ad uassalmēt la tre p̄chace
c um il des paens ad la guere fine
d e q̄ūkil ot fet ne fud chose cele
ꝑ la feste sen vunt chescon ē sa tere
h i ad nul q̄ ne ait de h. bone solde

l il aps ad vivū. a sun pere leisse
e ad Westir sa uerie lur turne
o d sun cosin modun ki ert rei de finee
ꝑ il li ad lembuur od gūt richesce donee
l altre ad sis compaīns hadeiof espusee
o d sa tre ētiture ke lur fud ottrie
w e Guedereche le rei ke sa mead mu ee
ꝑ ke la chose fud si tote p̄ale
l iluc suriornat tant cum lui agre
E nttant de soiorn cum iluc soiorna
Le vaillant haderiiod &. k'engendrat
k i affiche ēquist e q̄ p' regna
l ki tuz les peitz de paens uenga
w e pesce 7 de sen ētur le uitreat
c um cil p̄tat nitter ki la storie saura
j cest lais amun fiz Bilunot kil durrat
k il a rime ap mei biē cōtinera
e onuinues ert bon 7 de mei
o r reuenim a h. dunt cum il sen ala
e n sudden la gēt laiuulier amena
e mlt gūt tens od li bone vie mena
t ant ken richesce sa vie la fina
o r en die auant ki lestorie sauera
T omas nendurrat pl' tn autrē chanterat
T u autem domine miserere nostri

Tractat in lingua romana secundum dominum [illegible] episcopum de principio creacionis mundi. Et medio et fine. Et [illegible] mundi per peccatum. Et restauracione eius per [illegible]. Et [illegible] filio suo unigenito equali patri. Et .iiii. filiabus suis scilicet de [illegible] et veritate et iusticia et pace. Et de adventu ihesu christi [illegible] in quoddam castellum quod fuit corpus virginis intemerate marie. De [illegible] castelli. Et de prophecia [illegible] [illegible] [illegible] et filius [illegible] et vocabitur nomen eius admirabilis [illegible] pater futuri seculi princeps pacis [illegible] admirabilis [illegible] deus [illegible] fortis [illegible] pater futuri seculi et [illegible] princeps pacis. Et [illegible] de fine seculi et [illegible]. Et de penis inferni et de gaudiis celi. Et quamvis lingua romana coram clericis saporem suavitatis non habet tamen coram laicis qui minus intelligunt [illegible] [illegible] [illegible] lector qui [illegible] [illegible] [illegible] de [illegible] [illegible] [illegible] [illegible] [illegible] fidei [illegible] [illegible] [illegible] [illegible].

at St Mary, Osney, just outside Oxford. The poem's crusading rhetoric and moral teaching may, then, have been just as important to its early audience as its blood-and-guts action. *La Chanson de Roland*'s weighty style, its repetition and variation of key moments, its resolutely masculine and fervently Christian ethos, epitomize the French *chansons de geste*, which are traditionally contrasted with more individualist or lighthearted romances. However, these styles coexisted and intermingled: offshoots of the Charlemagne legend were indeed one of the most productive subjects for romance development. Much later, Roland re-emerges in *Orlando furioso* (1516), Ariosto's extravagant Italian romance mingling love, sorcery and a trip to the moon to recover Orlando's lost wits.

While *La Chanson de Roland* was reminding an ex-patriot Norman community of French heroism, stories about Britain were also taking hold, imaginatively reshaping these islands as a landscape of invasion and identity formation. The Anglo-Norman *Romance of Horn* (*c.*1170) is a prime example (fig. 13). The author names himself Thomas at the text's close, claiming that his son will continue the story of Horn's offspring:

> Icest lais a mun fiz, Gilimot, kil dirrat,
> Ki la rime apré mei bien controverat –
> Controvures ert bon: e de mei [ce retendra].[3]

> [I leave this to my son Wilmot to relate, who will compose the poem well following me – he will be a good poet: he inherits that from me.]

Thomas's self-confidence is justified by the richness of his story, and his command of the rhymed *laisse* form. The action revolves around mythicized versions of Britain, Britanny and Ireland. Young Horn is found by invading African warriors (whose role was probably played by Vikings in previous versions). His beauty inspires pity in the Saracen King Rodmund, who casts him and his companions out to sea rather than killing them. This familiar romance device of the sea journey, trusting to Fortune or God, allows Horn to land in Westernesse, the realm of King Hunlaf, where he grows up as a fine champion. The king's daughter Rigmel falls in love with him sight unseen. Her comic attempts to lure him to her chambers help to mark this text as romance, with audience expectations of female desire and young love as well as fighting:

> A ses puceles dit: 'Daunzeles, cum esta?
> Quel est or ma colur? cum se tient? cum s'en va?'
> Dient: 'Mut bien estait.' Chascune la loa. (lines 1022, 1022a, 1023)
>
> [She said to her women: 'Girls, how do I look? What is my colour like? Does it come and go?' They said: 'You look great' – each one praised her.]

Betrayed by the king's jealous steward, Horn escapes to Ireland, changing his name to Gudmod. His accomplishments in battle, at chess and in music win the heart of the Irish princess, but he remains loyal to Rigmel. Eventually he returns, rescuing her from the evil steward Wikele and expelling the Saracens from his ancestral lands. The climax comes when Horn, disguised as a pilgrim, enters the hall during a wedding feast for Wikele and the reluctant Rigmel. Horn asks Rigmel to pour him a drink. He drops the ring that symbolizes their love into the drinking horn, punning on his own name. She recognizes him and, Ulysses-like, he purges the hall and country of his enemies. Drinking and hunting horns were commonly used to symbolize land rights or commemorate family relationships, and so Horn's merging of his own identity with that of the horn is a fitting extension of romance's ability to mingle telling objects with the people who use them (fig. 14).

The narrative tendrils of *The Romance of Horn* spread throughout the areas touched by Anglo-Norman power, and so bind them into an Insular mythology of miraculous survivals, meteoric rises and falls, and the establishment of landed power. At the likely time of its composition, for example, Henry II was keen to solidify Angevin influence in Ireland. The king was in Dublin over Christmas 1171, visiting Richard FitzGilbert of Clare, an adventurer nicknamed Strongbow whom the king made tenant-in-chief of Leinster. In this context of a developing English state seeking to impose rule over Wales, Ireland and Scotland, Horn's ability to win over kings and princesses, and the poem's focus on unswerving loyalty at a distance, are telling parables of England's emerging imperial ambitions. King Henry and Strongbow would have been appropriate listeners to *The Romance of Horn*'s dramatic lessons in love and statecraft.

The Romance of Horn provides another example of power relationships at work, this time on a cultural level. Having taken its plotline probably from an Insular legend, it is one of many Anglo-Norman and French romances translated or adapted into English – a linguistic interplay that continued throughout the Middle Ages.

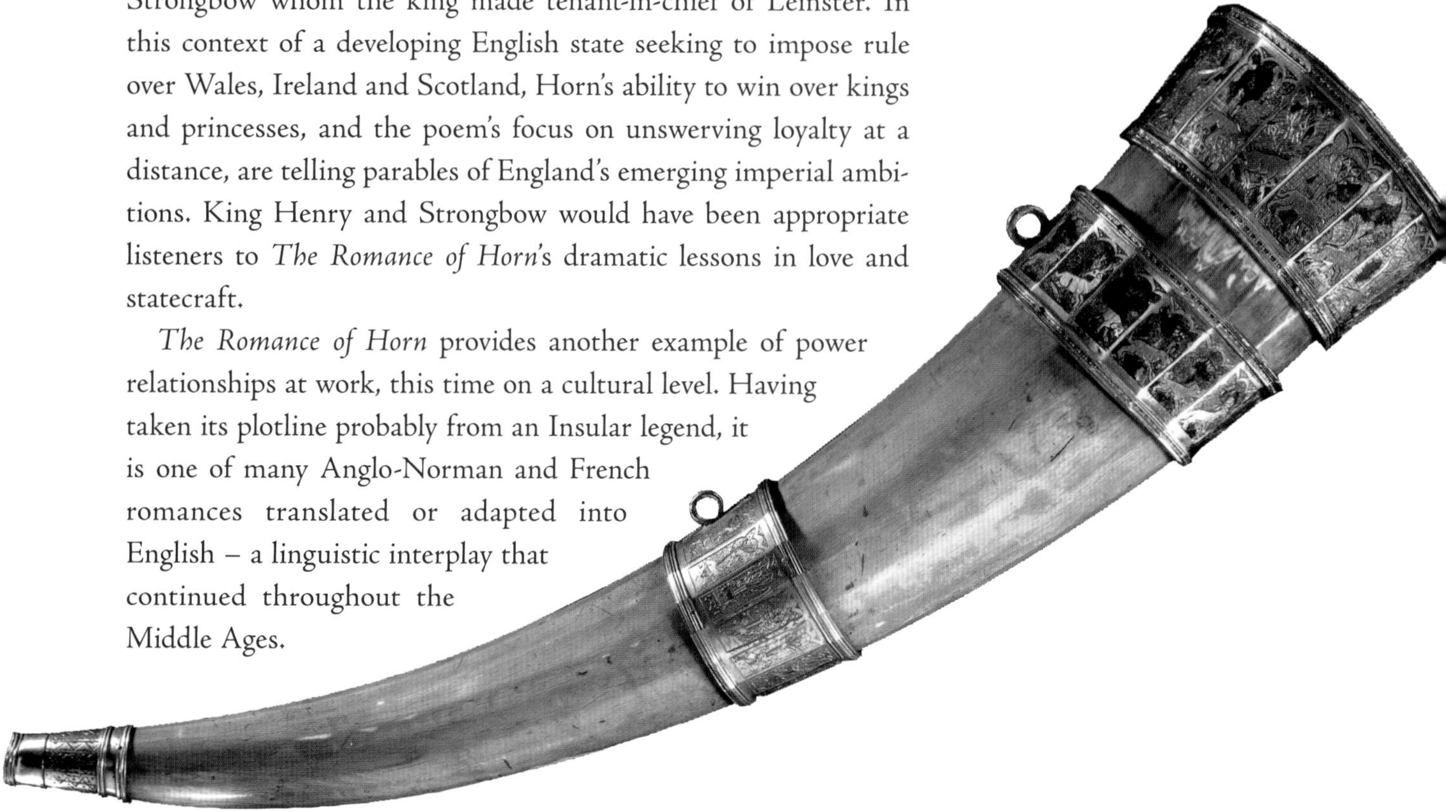

Figure 14. The Savernake Horn has been associated with the Savernake Forest in Wiltshire and its owners, the Seymour family, since at least Elizabethan times, when King Henry VIII hunted there and married Sir John Seymour's daughter Jane. The decorative bands near the horn's mouth date from the fourteenth century, and are carved with creatures including hawks, a unicorn and a lion. On the upper band are depicted a king apparently conversing with a bishop, while a forester stands by them. London, British Museum, M&ME 1975.4-1,1. © Trustees of the British Museum.

Horn, the English version of *The Romance of Horn*, follows its source text's outline, but its style is markedly pared back, with short rhyming couplets replacing the French text's voluptuous Alexandrine lines:

> 'Quen, so swete and dere, *Queen*
> Ich am Horn thin oghe. *own*
> Ne canstu me noght knowe? *Can't you recognize me?*
> Ich am Horn of Westernesse;
> In armes thu me cusse.'
> Hi custe hem mid ywisse *They kissed one another*
> And makeden muche blisse.[4]

The simplicity (some have said naivety) of *Horn*'s style allows a powerful focus on moments essential to the narrative. Like most medieval translations, this is also a transformation for a new audience with altered cultural horizons and priorities.

Alongside *Horn* in Bodleian Library, MS Laud Misc. 108 is *Havelok*, another story adapted from Anglo-Norman and with a plot circling around Britain. Havelok is a Danish prince exiled in England, raised incognito by the fisherman Grim. A treacherous regent, Godrich, forces the English princess Goldboru to marry Havelok. Godrich thinks that he has ruined her prospects by matching her with a fisherman's lad, but at night she sees a blazing light emanating from Havelok's mouth, and hears from an angelic voice that he is destined to rule Denmark and England. *Havelok* mingles the historical fluidity of relations between Scandinavia and England, a rags-to-riches adventure, and God-inspired destiny. It satisfies a desire for origin stories that smooth the jagged edges of invasion and conquest, and makes its protagonist a religious hero rivalling the

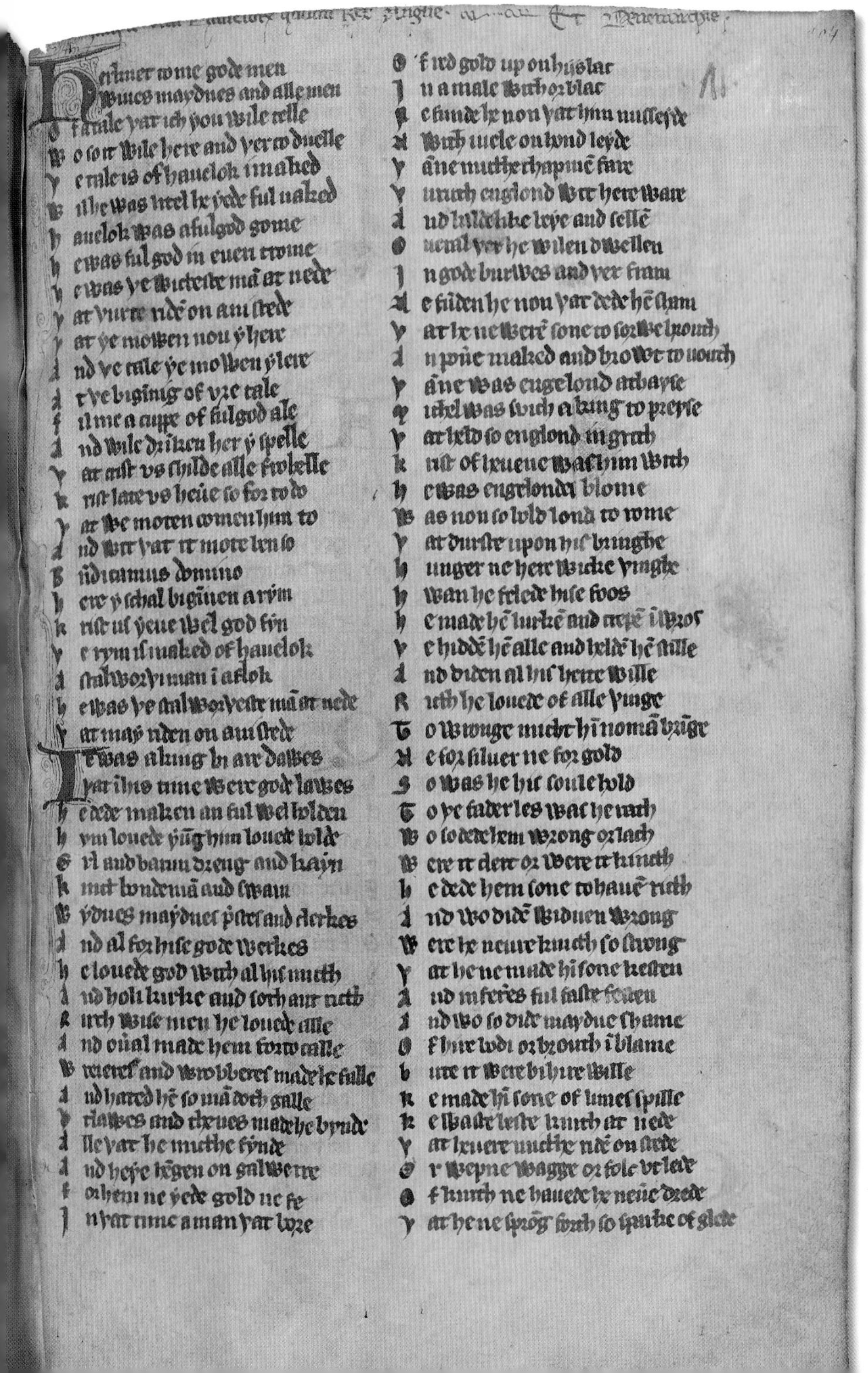

Figure 15. *Havelok* is one of the earliest surviving English romances, extant only in this copy. The scribe seems unfamiliar with English spelling, causing him problems in reproducing some sounds and letter forms. *Havelok* and *Horn* are compiled with numerous saints' lives here, shaping this collection as a series of royal and religious biographies. Oxford, Bodleian Library, MS Laud Misc. 108, fol. 204r (England, *c.* 1300–1325).

saints' lives bound together with *Horn* and *Havelok* in MS Laud Misc. 108. A headnote to *Havelok* calls it a *vita*, the usual heading for hagiography: 'Incipit vita Hauelok quondam rex Anglie et Denemarchie' (Here begins the life of Havelok, once king of England and Denmark: fig. 15). The thirteenth-century seal of the town of Grimsby depicts Grim with Havelok and Goldboru as testament to this story's value as a myth of origins (Grimsby seal, fig. 16). MS Laud Misc. 108, one of the earliest manuscripts containing romances in English, blends a tone of exemplary morality with these stories of conquest and settlement.

Romance's ability to imagine possible worlds, pushing at geographical and temporal limits, is one of its energizing forces. Hence romance versions of classical myths forge connections between the pre-Christian Mediterranean and contemporary crises of religion and governance. The Troy narrative is especially inviting, combining a lengthy siege with space for sub-plots, rivalries, the meddling gods, and reflections on the cost of Middle Eastern campaigns at a time when the Crusades sapped money and men on all sides. The *Laud Troy Book* (Bodleian Library, MS Laud Misc. 595: fig. 17) opens grandly by evoking other romance heroes, including Roland, Gawain, Tristram, Richard the Lionheart, Havelok and Horn, before claiming tendentiously that the Trojan story of Hector and Achilles does not receive enough attention:

Figure 16. The Grimsby town seal depicts the three main protagonists of the Havelok legend: Grim the fisherman in the centre, with Havelok on the left and Goldboru on the right. The original engraved metal matrix dates from the thirteenth century. Wax impression of Grimsby seal, North East Lincolnshire Archives ref. 1/942/1.

Alle myghty god in trinite
Sothfaste god in persones thre
Fadir sone and holi gost
In whom is witte and myghtes most
Be at this tale begynnyng
And also at the endyng
So ende oure tale and so bygynne
The ioye of heuene al for to wynne
After oure lyff at oure laste ende
To ioye of heuene alle for to wende
Many speken of men that romaunces rede
That were sumtyme doughti in dede
The while that god hem lyff lente
That now ben dede and hennes wente
Off Bevis Gy and of Gawayn
Off kyng Richard & of Owayn
Off Tristram and of Percyuale.
Off Rouland Ris and Agaulale
Off Archeroun and of Octouian
Of Charles & of Cassibaldan
Off Hauelok Horne & of Wade
In romaunces that of hem ben made
That gestoures often dos of hem gestes
At mangeres and at grete ffestes
Here dedis ben in remembraunce
In many fair romaunce
But of the worthiest wyght in wede
That euere bystrod any stede
Spekes no man ne in romaunce redes
Off his batayle ne of his dedis
Off that batayle spekes no man
There alle prowes of knyghtes be gan

Here dedis ben in remembranunce — *Their deeds*
In many fair Romaunce;
But of the worthiest wyght in wede — *worthiest man on earth [Hector]*
That euere by-strod any stede, — *That ever rode a horse*
Spekes no man, ne in romaunce redes
Off his batayle ne of his dedis.[5]

Troy was both a doomed city and an embryonic empire because of Aeneas's escape to found a Roman dynasty. There was even a popular story that Britain was named after another Trojan evacuee, Brutus. London was sometimes called Troynovant – New Troy – and the extravagant King Richard II compared to Troilus. The *Gawain*-Poet enjoys the cachet of Britain's imperial Trojan inheritance, but also connects it with unexpected disasters:

And fer ouer þe French flod, Felix Brutus
On mony bonkkes ful brode Bretayn he settez
    Wyth wynne,
  Where were and wrake and wonder
  Bi syþez hatz wont þerinne
  And oft boþe blysse and blunder
  Ful skete hatz skyfted synne.[6]

[And from far across the French sea, Felix Brutus founded Britain on many broad hills, with joy; where war, revenge and wonder have taken place at times, and often delight and ruin have shifted back and forth.]

Figure 17. The grand opening of *The Laud Troy Book* cites famous romance heroes from Gawain to Horn and Havelok. Its seventeenth-century owner Archbishop Laud (1573–1645), Chancellor of Oxford University, has inscribed his name underneath, adding notes on the text above and a shelfmark, K. 76, assigning the manuscript its place in his personal library. Oxford, Bodleian Library, MS Laud Misc. 595, fol. 1r (England, early fifteenth century).

Although Troy provides examples of the finest knightly behaviour, the story rests on twin poles of lust (the seizure of Helen by Paris) and treachery (the notorious Trojan Horse). Besieged cities, with the politics and casualties surrounding them, were familiar to medieval audiences (fig. 18). For writers on Troy, often members fort doubteuse vne telle entreprinse. et que par auenture de ce ne fust cer tainement courroussee bri seyda pour quoy honte et diffame luy en suruint. Et en telle maniere auti neffois voullant luy et lautre non. puis pensoit vne chose puis lautre ainsi estoit entre deux le gentil amoreux et gracieux s[ir]e tant comme il estoit en

ceste facon furent prins plusieurs parlemens qui estoient entre les barons de ce que faisoit besoing pour les matieres lors proposees Et tout debatu fut conclud et dit la res ponce faitte a ceulx des grecz qui lattendoient que briseyda seroit deliuree baillee et rendue et que jamais par eulx nauoit este detenue.

Tout ainsi que la grant challeur du souleil et lasp

chault qui vient es mois de juillet et daoust abat

of a clerical cadre, the narrative also raised problems of historical perspective: all the protagonists were doomed to hell as pagans, yet their story spoke directly to the dilemmas of contemporary empire and human relations. In *Troilus and Criseyde* (1380s) Geoffrey Chaucer addresses this issue directly, imagining the past as a foreign country and finding not merely that they do things differently there, but proposing that this difference is trivial compared to underlying continuities:

Ye know eek that in forme of speche is chaunge — *also*
Withinne a thousand yeer, and wordes tho — *then*
That hadden pris, now wonder nyce and straunge — *value* / *barbarous and strange*
Us thinketh hem, and yet thei spake hem so,
And spedde as wel in love as men now do.[7] — *acted/got on*

The tragic love of Troilus and Criseyde, a synecdoche of the whole Troy legend, enables Chaucer to examine belief, trust, desire and power at different levels of magnification, finding threads that link them: from the subtlest gestures and looks of the young lovers to the fateful decisions of kings and gods. One of the sixteen surviving manuscripts of *Troilus and Criseyde* was copied for the Scottish aristocrat Henry, Lord Sinclair, who died fighting the English at Flodden Field in 1513 (Bodleian Library, MS Arch. Selden. B. 24: fig. 45). The manuscript contains other Chaucerian and Scottish texts and *The Kingis Quair*, a dream-vision poem by King James I of Scotland. Its large format and aristocratic patronage suggest the serious attention paid to Chaucer's work in fifteenth-century Scotland, both as a cultural status symbol and as a store of knowledge

Figure 18. This richly illustrated manuscript contains a French prose adaptation of Boccaccio's *Il filostrato*: the *Roman de Troÿle* by Pierre de Beauveau. In this scene, King Priam makes the fateful decision to exchange Criseyde for Antenor (who will later betray Troy to the Greeks). Oxford, Bodleian Library, MS Douce 331, fol. 35r (France, *c.* 1350–1375).

about love, politics and history.[8] Another Bodleian manuscript, MS Douce 148, contains John Lydgate's *Troy Book* (written for King Henry V between 1412 and 1420) adapted to form a Scottish Troy text. These Scottish manuscripts of romance and mythic empires also document complex national and regional relationships at work in medieval Britain.

Sometimes Troy narratives were compiled with stories of other imperilled cities to emphasize historical parallels and press more contemporary agendas. Bodleian Library, MS Digby 230 includes Lydgate's *Troy Book*, his *Siege of Thebes* (framed as a Canterbury tale, with Lydgate muscling in on the pilgrim company to fill the gaps left by Chaucer's Theban *Knight's Tale*), and *Titus and Vespasian*, a poem concerning the Roman siege of Jerusalem in AD 70. Violently anti-Semitic, the poem views the sack of Jerusalem as revenge for Christ's death. Whereas the stories of Troy and Thebes were perceived as part of the turning motion of Fortune's wheel, this siege becomes part of God's plan to establish a Christian empire. By the late thirteenth century, this vision was in trouble after the repeated disappointments of the Crusades. Nevertheless, history and romance writing continued to dwell on the fears and desires of Western audiences: fears about Jews, Muslims and heretics; desire for their assimilation or destruction. In *Richard Coeur de Lyon*, Richard the Lionheart's campaigns are described in a mixture of fictionalized chronicle and the narrative exuberance of romance. The picture initiating this text in the Auchinleck Manuscript (fig. 26) shows a giant-sized Richard wielding a huge axe as he leads his men on a seaborne assault. In the poem, Richard is cured of illness by eating the pork-like flesh of a captured Saracen. Nicola

McDonald has persuasively suggested that the romance operates an 'alimentary logic', where starvation, scavenging and cannibalism all become grist to the conflict between Christians and Muslims. Rapacious hunger of all kinds often emerges in medieval texts about empire, linking the bodily appetites of rulers to the extension or excretions of the body politic.[9] Later, Richard orders that a group of Saracen envoys be served with the cooked heads of their compatriots, complete with name tags. This grotesque scene – a variation on the medieval penchant for exotic and sculptural foods served at royal banquets – might also remind us of the decapitated head in *Sir Gawain and the Green Knight*, which, unlike these boiled and spiced victims, talks back at the complacent Arthurian court.

While equally indebted to shocking special effects, *The King of Tars* imagines a 'happier' ending to a Christian–Saracen encounter. A Christian princess reluctantly marries a Saracen sultan to avert war. They have a child, but

> lim no hadde it non. *it had no limbs*
> Bot as a rond of flesche yschore *cut/carved*
> In a chaumber it lay hem before
> Wiþouten blod and bon.[10]

The sultan's gods are no help (Christian texts often misdescribe Islam as polytheistic, associating it with classical paganism). However, the princess has a Christian priest baptise the lump-child, who is miraculously transformed into a healthy baby. The sultan converts, and at baptism his black skin becomes white. *The King of Tars* appears between *The Legend of Pope Gregory* and *The Life of Adam and Eve*, early in the Auchinleck Manuscript, and also features in the Vernon Manuscript (fig. 29). Its racial and religious stereotyping reinforces Christian doctrine on prayer, miracles, conversion, and the sacrament of baptism; its elements of comedy and curiosity about other faiths and cultures are also significant, however, as part of a patchwork of medieval engagement with the peoples challenging Western European territory and philosophy. Analogous stories circulated about Christians converting to Islam, for example 'The Muslim Champion and the Christian Damsel' from the *One Thousand and One Nights*. Whether reframing the past, redrawing maps of conquest and conversion, or reflecting on the power of women and men to change the course of history, romances demonstrate a rich spatial and temporal imagination that interacts unpredictably with more conventional accounts of nations or empires.

Amidst the space dedicated to expansionist power and the strong rulership that secures it, medieval narratives contemplate the ends of empire: that is, its purpose, its limits and its decline. Sometimes a marginal irritation or infelicity moves into the centre, which we then realize is already decaying. This discovery resonates with Christian teaching that earth's proud empires will pass away. Arthurian narratives repeatedly invoke such contrasts. Arthur is boldly challenging the Roman emperor in Geoffrey of Monmouth's *The History of the Kings of Britain* when he is betrayed by his nephew Mordred, leading to internecine war and a mortally wounded Arthur being carried to the Isle of Avalon. Geoffrey's work gained huge popularity, generating heated debates over the truth of the stories, the locations and monuments associated with them, and the dangerously political prophecies of Arthur's return. Indeed, King Henry VII named his

Figure 19. The Red Book of Hergest is one of the most important books written in Welsh. One of its scribes has been identified as Hywel Fychan fab Hywel Goch of Buellt. The book was possibly compiled for Hopcyn ap Tomas ab Einion of Ynysforgan, near Swansea. The Arthurian romance *Owein*, or *Iarlles y Fyynnawn* (*The Lady of the Fountain*) starts on this folio. Oxford, Jesus College MS 111, fol. 154v (Wales, *c.* 1380–1410). © The Principal and Fellows of Jesus College, Oxford.

Yr amherawdyr arthur oed yg
kaerllion ar wysc. Sef yd oed
yn eisted diwarnawt yn y ystau
uell. ac gyt ac ef owein uab
uryen. a chynon uab clydno. a
chei uab kynyr. a gwenhwyuar ae
llawuorynyon yn gwniaw wrth ffenestyr.
a chyt dywettit uot porthawr ar lys
arthur. nyt oed yr un. Glewlwyt ga
uaelawr oed yno hagen ar ureint por
thawr y aruoll ysp a phellennigyon.
ac y dechreu eu hanrydedu. ac y uene
gi moes y llys ac deuawt udunt. yr
neb a dylyei uynet yr neuad neu yr ys
tauell oe uenegi idaw. yr neb a dylyei
letty oe uenegi idaw. Ac ymperued llawr
yr ystauell yd oed yr amherawdyr arth
yn eisted. ar demyl o irvrwyn a llenn
o bali melyngoch y danaw. a gobennyd
a dudet o bali coch dan penn y elin.
A chymmy y dywawt arthur. Ha wyr
yr pei nam goganewch heb ef mi a
gysgwn tra uewn yn aros vym bwyt.
ac ymdidan a ellwch chwitheu. a chym
ryt ystenneit o ued a golwython y gan
gei. a chysgu a oruc yr amherawdyr.
A gofyn a oruc kynon uab klydno y gei yr
hynn a adawssei arthur udunt.
A minneu a vynnaf yr ymdidan da
ac edewit y minneu heb y kei. Ha wr
heb y kynon tecach yw itti dwyn edewit
arthur yn gyntaf. ac odyna
yr ymdidan goreu a wypom ninneu
ni ae dywedwn itti. Mynet a oruc kei
yr gegin. ac yr vedgell. a dyuot ac ys
tenneit o ved gantaw. ac a gorflwch
eur. ac a llonneit y dwrn o ueryeu. a golw
ython arnadunt. A chymryt y golw
ython a wnaethant. a dechreu yuet
y med. Weithon heb y kei chwitheu
bieu talu y minneu uy ymdidan.
Kynon heb yr owein tal y ymdidan
y gei. Dioer heb y kynon hyn gwr yw

or hynn odidockaf a wypych. a mi a wnaf
heb y kynon. Mi a uum yn mab mam a
that oedwn i. a drythyll oedwn. a mawr
oed vy rwyf. Ac ny thybygwn uyn byt
a orffei arnaf o neb ryw gamhwri. A gwe
dy daruot im goruot ar bob camhwri or
a oed yn vn wlat a mi. Ymgyweiraw a w
neuthum a cherdet eithauoed byt a di
ffeithwch. Ac ym diwed. Ac ym diwed
dyhamwein a wneuthum ar y glynn tecaf
yn y byt. a gwyd gogyfuch yndaw. Ac a fo
rygedawc oed ar hyt y glynn. a ffordd gan
ystlys yr auon. a cherdet y ffordd a wne
uthum hyt hanner dyd. Ar parth arall
a gerdeis hyt prytnawn. A chyrchu y deu
thum y maes mawr. ac yn diwed y ma
es yd oed kaer uawr lywychedic. a gweil
gi yn gyfagos yr gaer. a pharth ar gaer
y deuthum. Ac nachaf y gwelwn deu
was pengrych velyn. a ractal eur am
penn pob un ohonunt. A pheis o bali
melyn am bop un onadunt. a gwaegeu
eur am bwngleu eu traet ymeu traet.
A bwa o asgwrn eliphant yn llaw pob un
onadunt. Ac eu llinynneu o ieu hyd.
Ac saetheu ac eu peleidyr o asgwrn moruil.
gwedy eu hasgellu ac adaned paun. A
phenneu eur ar y peleidyr. A chyllell a
llafneu eur udunt. Ac eu karneu o asgwrn
moruil yn nodeu udunt. Ac y byrwn yn
saethu eu kyllell. A rynnaw y wrthunt
y gwelwn gwr pengrych melyn yn y dewred.
ac uaryf ynnewyd eillaw. A pheis a man
tell o pali melyn ymdanaw. ac ysnoden
o eurllin ympenn y uantell. a dwy wim
tas o gordwal brith am y draet. a deu
gnap o eur yn eu kaeu. A phan y gweleis
i e nessau a wneuthum [illegible]. a
chyfarch gwell a wneuthum idaw. Ac rac
dahet y gyfwot ef. kynt y kyuarchawd
ef well ym no minneu idaw ef. A dyuot
gyt a mi a oruc parth ar gaer. Ac nyt
oed gyuanhed yn y gaer. namyn a oed

heir Arthur; only his premature death brought Arthur's younger brother to the throne as Henry VIII.

King Arthur, then, was Britain's equivalent to Charlemagne and Alexander the Great. He appears in this company in one of the most important documents of Welsh literature, the Red Book of Hergest (Oxford, Jesus College MS 111), which was compiled *c.*1380–1410. This impressive volume of more than 350 folios presents a compendium of mythology, history, romance and lyric poetry (fig. 19).[11] Versions of the Troy legend and Geoffrey of Monmouth are followed by chronicles of Welsh princes, and Gildas's excoriating address to Welsh leaders during the Saxon conquests, *De excidio Britanniae* (*The Ruin of Britain*). It then moves on to Charlemagne and Roland, poems on Welsh history, romances, the legends of the *Mabinogion*, medical and advisory texts, and other poetry. In this company, Arthur's narrative acts as an exemplary instance of human greatness and its limitations. Romance versions of the Arthurian legends can also carry a critique of Arthur as expansionist ruler. One example is the northern English *Awntyrs off Arthur* (*The Adventures of Arthur*). Its second part relates how Gawain is challenged by Galeron, whose estates Arthur has 'wonun … in werre with a wrange wile / And geven hem to Sir Gawayn – that my hert grylles' (gained in war with an unjust trick and given them to Sir Gawain – that angers me at heart).[12] Eventually Gawain defeats Galeron but returns his lands. This accommodation of a threatening external force restores order. However, Arthur's new gifts to Gawain – 'The worship of Wales at wil and at wolde' (line 666: the lordship of Wales under his authority) – indicates that there are always losers in imperial projects, and challenges lords to deal fairly with their vassals.

Figure 20. The first part of *The Awntyrs off Arthur* tells of the revenant corpse of Guinevere's mother warning her daughter and Gawain about the sinful lives of the knightly class. The poet employs alliteration and rhyme; the shorter lines rounding off each stanza are marked with red links, a common practice in English manuscripts. Oxford, Bodleian Library, MS Douce 324, fol. 1r (England, *c.*1450–1475).

In the tyme of Arthur an aunter bytydde
By þe Turnewathelan as þe boke telles
Whan he to Carlele was comen and conquerour kydde
With Dukes and dussiperes þat with þe dere dwelles
To hunte at þe herdes þat longe had ben hydde
On a day þei hem dight to þe depe delles
To fall of þe femailes in forest and frydde
ffayre by þe firmysthamis in frithes and felles
Thus to wode arn þei went þe wlonkest in wedes
Bothe þe kyng and þe quene
And al þe doughti bydene
Sir Gawayn gayest on grene
Dame Gaynour he ledes

Thus Sir Gawayn þe gay Gaynour he ledes
In a gleterand gide þat glemed full gay
With riche ribaynes reversset ho so right redes
Rayled with rybees of riall array
Her hode of a herde huwe þat her hede hedes
Of pillour of palwerk of perre to pay
Schurde in a short cloke þat þe rayne shedes
Set over with saffres soþely to say
With saffres and seladynes set by þe sides
Here sadel sette of þat ilke
Saude with sambutes of silke
On a mule as þe mylke
Gaili she glides

Al in gleterand golde gayly ho glides
Þe gates with Sir Gawayn bi þe grene welle
And þat burne on his blonke with þe quene bides
Þat borne was in Borgoyne by boke and by belle
He ladde þat lady so longe by þe lawe sides
Under a lorre þey light loȝe by a felle

بدارند بر جای خویش استوار | خود از جای جنبید شوریده وار
ببالین گو خسته آمد فراز | ز درع کیانی گره کرد باز
سر خسته را بر سر ران نهاد | شب تیره بر روز رخشان نهاد

فرو بسته چشم آن تن خوابناک | بدو گفت بد خیز ازین خون و خاک
رها کن که در من رهایی نماند | چراغ مرا روشنایی نماند
بهرام بد آن کو نه پهلو درید | که شد در جگر پهلویم ناپدید
تو ای پهلوان گاهی پهلوی من | نگه دار پهلو ز پهلوی من
که با این که پهلو دریدم چو میغ | همی آید از پهلویم بوی تیغ
سر سرور از زار ها کن ز دست | تو مشکن که یاران خود شکست

A sense of foreboding is established by part I of *Awntyrs*, in which Gawain and Guinevere are confronted by a grisly phantom: the revenant corpse of the queen's mother. Gawain asks the apparition: 'How shal we fare … that fonden to fight, / And thus defoulen the folke on fele kinges londes[?]' (lines 261–2: What will happen to us, who stir up this conflict and oppress the people in many kingdoms?). Her answer predicts Arthur's fall, as soon as Fortune's wheel turns. While few Arthurian romances so explicitly point a putrifying finger at the ambitions of empire, many contain implicit warnings. Bodleian Library, MS Douce 324 contains the *Awntyrs*, but was once bound with at least two other Bodleian books, MS Rawl. D. 82 and MS Rawl. poet. 168 (fig. 20). The former includes prose accounts of the Sieges of Troy and Thebes; the latter contains Thomas Hoccleve's advice poem to the future King Henry V, *The Regiment of Princes*. All these texts encourage serious reflection on the duties as well as the glories of rulership.

Finally, we shall turn to the Alexander texts contained in Bodleian Library, MS Bodl. 264, a book that epitomizes the shifting power relations encountered in this chapter. Initially a Flemish production, its astonishingly rich illustrations were completed in 1344 by the artist Jehan de Grise (fig. 9). The French *Roman d'Alexandre* is expanded by continuations that introduce chivalric adventures, vows and complex subplots, creating an encyclopaedic Alexander compilation. By the early fifteenth century, the manuscript was in England, part of a continuing influx of high-quality continental books serving the French-speaking aristocracy. Other texts and pictures were added, including the English alliterative poem *Alexander and Dindimus*, and a French work about Marco

Figure 21. In this beautifully balanced illustration from Nizami's *Iskandar-nama*, Iskandar (Alexander the Great) comforts the dying Dara (Darius of Persia), who has been treacherously wounded by two of his own officers. Oxford, Bodleian Library, MS Elliott 192, fol. 251r (Persia, 1500–1501).

Polo, which echoes the Alexander texts' interest in exploring the world's margins.

For medieval readers, Alexander stands as the ultimate imperial figure, who conquered the known world and around whom a host of stories developed, not only about his military prowess, but concerning his conception and childhood, tutoring by Aristotle (see fig. 44), discovery of natural wonders, attempt to become immortal, and supposed death from poison. Alexander (or Iskandar) was also a key figure for Persian narratives such as Firdausi's epic *Shahnama* (completed AD 1010) and the later romance *Iskandarnama* (late twelfth or early thirteenth century), among the five narrative poems known together as the *Khamsa*, by Nizami. To mitigate the embarrassment of this Macedonian leader playing so central a part in Persian history, Iskandar was claimed to have Iranian blood. Aside from his military and political achievements (fig. 21), Iskandar also becomes a philosopher-ruler, whose adventures reflect on his mortality. In *Shahnama*, for example, he discovers a wondrous talking tree near the world's edge. One of its trunks is male, and speaks during the day. The other is female, and speaks at night (fig. 22). The tree foretells Iskandar's death, telling him that he will never see his native land again. This key symbolic shift – the great emperor facing the limits of his power – is developed in *Alexander and Dindimus*, the English poem added to MS Bodl. 264. A note on fol. 67r asks readers to turn forwards to this text to fill gaps in the French narrative. What the English poem provides, however, is a philosophical debate between Alexander's active, destructive, polytheistic lifestyle and the contemplative, self-contained, monotheistic creed of

Figure 22. A telling full-page illustration from Firdausi's epic *Shahnama* depicts Iskandar with the talking tree which foretells his death. The female speaking head indicates a night-time setting, while the animal heads may refer to the tree's penchant for devouring wild animals left for it as sacrifices. This manuscript was commissioned for the Timurid prince Ibrahim Sultan, grandson of the great conqueror Timur (Tamerlane). Oxford, Bodleian Library, MS Ouseley Add. 176, fol. 311v (Shiraz, Iran, *c.* 1430).

the Brahmans and their king, Dindimus (fig. 23), who reproves the imperial leader in a letter:

> Alle ȝe vsen vnrith and after þat wirchen;
> ȝe ben luþur of ȝour lif and lawus ȝe chaunge.
> Of more make ȝe auaunt þan ȝe mow forþen;
> Wis holde ȝe no whi but ȝif he wel conne
> Faire tempren his tounge his tale to schew.[13] (568–72)

> [You all behave unlawfully and work in that fashion; your way of life is wicked and you alter the laws. You boast far more than ever you can achieve; You think no-one wise unless he knows well to flatter with his language when he spins you a story.]

Although Alexander replies that the Brahmans' poverty should be pitied, not emulated, he does not attempt to conquer them. Instead he has a pillar of marble built at this symbolic border. The accompanying illustration depicts Alexander with one leg made of stone. Ozymandias-like, the picture serves as a warning that the most monumental rulers are still vulnerable – something that the manuscript's later owner Richard Woodville, Earl Rivers (beheaded in 1469 on the orders of Richard Neville, 'Warwick the Kingmaker'), would have done well to heed. In its imaginative reach and ambivalent dealings with all kinds of empires, then, medieval romance maps changing patterns of power and cultural interaction both within its compelling narratives and beyond them to its writers, patrons and audiences.

Figure 23. The alliterative poem *Alexander and Dindimus* was added to MS Bodl. 264 in England early in the fifteenth century. Here Alexander's destructive lifestyle is condemned by Dindimus and his Brahman followers. Their nakedness is partially covered by floreate decoration, also suggesting their status as natural beings untarnished by pride and greed. Oxford, Bodleian Library, MS Bodl. 264, fol. 212r (England, early fifteenth century).

Hit is noht long in us lud þei hit loþ seme.
For I haue sent þe my sondes as þou þi self bade.
But be þou noht bolde king balful no tened.
Þat þou miht tyþli tyþe þe trewest lawe.
For we schulle minge þe many swiche maner lores.
Þat þou miht liþliche lud þe beste lawe kenne.
Whan þou hit wisliche wost whine hit in herte.
& lowe þi lordschipe & þi lif mende.
Asie & Aufrik & Europ þe grete.
Þou hast lowed to þe lud in a litil while.
Þe leem of þe sonne liht þou lettest to schine.
So brem bringest þou þi men alle in bryht armures.
& þe gulden ger þat þi gomes usen.
Wiþ þe blasinge ble blenden þe sonne.
Þou hast lowed wiþ þi rout þi riche stedus.
Þere þe grauel of þe grounde was of gold ore.
Þat on was called Ciron & þat oþer large.
Þe peple callede Pactolus þat þou pore madest.
So fale folewen þe folk to fonde þi heste.
Þat was hure drinkinke draht whan þei drie þirsten.
Ȝe maken stinte of his strem a stude ful huge.
Þat Nilus þe noble flod nammed is wide.
So muche holdest þou þe man of miht & of strenkþe.
Þat þou miht ouer ocean wiþ þin ost saile.
So wis wenest þou þe be þat þou by wit mihtest.
Þorou þi maistrie muche make to slepe.
& Cerberus þe helle hound þat holden is kene.
Þe ope wakrong & wikke & wardein of paine.
Ȝe ne fonde no fast but fillen ȝoure wombis.
Eten euere whan ȝe list & in ese libben.
Unkinde kiþe ȝe ȝou to kille ȝoure children.
To queme quedfulle goddes þat quenchen ȝour blisse.
& to ȝoure sonoram of sinne sacrifice maken.
Wiþ þat unblisful blod þat þei bled hauen.
Muche maugre ȝe maken among many kingus.
& gret werre in þis world to waste þe peple.
Many men up on molde ful meke & ful simple.
Þorou þe prince pride ful proude ben wore.
Ȝe wene winne noht inow on þis worlde one.
But ȝif ȝe heuene miht haue & holden hit alse.
Michel gilte ȝe gonne bi ȝour goddes false.
As þei were woned in þis world to wurchen in hure liue.
For ensample bi my sawe soþ mowe ȝe fonge.
Of Iubiter þe ioliest iugged to þinne
He was alosed in his lif lechours of kinde.

He hadde while he here was to hordom ieged.
Siþ won in þis world of wommen aliue.
For þei ȝe holde him a god þat in helle lengeþ.
& þat sorwful sinne for his sake usen.
Þ proue hit by Proserpine þat ȝe praisen alle.
& holden goddesse god to giuen ȝou here
Hure was lecherie lif þe while hue liuede alse.
& many lud by hure lay hur lust to fulfille.
Many men upon molde made hure by sliþe.
To haunte hure in hordom hur hole lif time.
Of hure terful tach ȝe taken ensample.
Þat any while hure wone in werkes to fonde.

How he swareþ not Alexandre to telle him of his gouernaunce.

Alle ȝe usen unriȝthand and aftur þat wurchen. ȝe ben lipper of ȝour lif & lawes ȝe chaunge. Of more make ȝe anaunt þan ȝe mowe forþen. Þis holde ȝe no wit but ȝif he wel conne. Faire tempren his tounge his tale to schewe.
Muche matere of wit mingeþ ȝour tounge.
But best holde I a burn þat bereþ him al stille.
Ȝe geden ȝou gret won of gold & of silver.
& muche liken ȝou lache lordliche holdes.
& siþen many seruauntis ȝou silue to alowe.
To be kettere ikid þan any kouþ peple.
& ȝit þe liue þat ȝe liue þorou lasse fode.
Þan oþer seggus þat semen simple murthe
Of richesse & of renoun ronne be ȝe kidde.
& ben baldere iwis þan any burn elles
But oure kinde kominge ȝou ouer comeþ nouþe.
In alle dedes þat ȝe don in ȝoure daies time.
We witen weies ful wel þat ȝe were alle.
Bremliche ibrouht forþ & bred of þat modur

Thow schalt in word be trewe also
And wytnes fals schalt þou none bere
Whethyr þou make þi frend no foo
Loke þou [illegible] full gretly here
Thy neyghbor wyff þou noyght desyre
Ne womman non [illegible] coveyt
But as holy chyrch wold it were
Right so þi [illegible] loke þou folow
House ne lond ne oþer thing
Thou schall not coveyt wrongfully
But kepe well [illegible] god bidding
And [illegible] feyth love stedfastly
These ben þe comandmentes x
Þat come [illegible] in þe [illegible]
That god gaff [illegible]
Them to kepe [illegible] for to here
In [illegible] [illegible] nyght
To helpe mannes kynd forth of [illegible]
[illegible] þe hond of god all myght
To eche man kynd þat [illegible]
All þat [illegible] þese commaundmentes kepe
In heven wt god schall [illegible]
Iff þat they well [illegible] them kepe
[illegible]

Amen quod Kate

Chapter 3

Alison Wiggins

Scribes *and* Settings

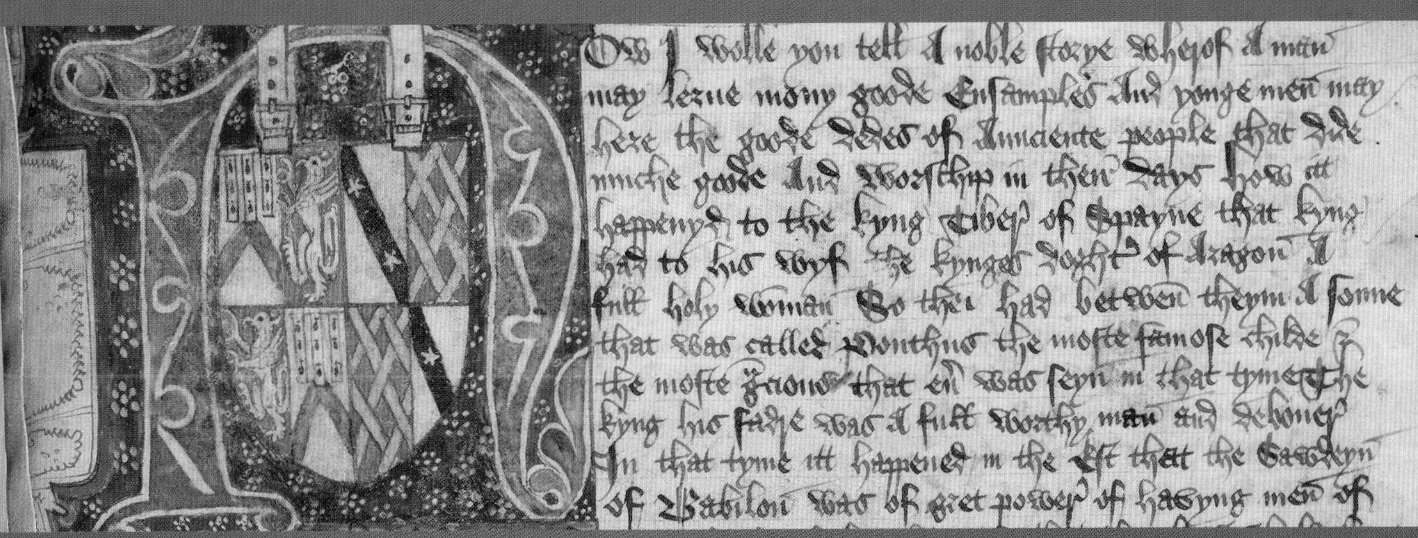

MEDIEVAL ROMANCES can be found among the pages of some of the largest, most lavishly decorated and carefully executed books in the Bodleian Library, but they also appear in some of the smallest, most modest, humble and haphazard productions. From magnificent vellum tomes to cheap, flimsy, paper pamphlets, the great diversity of handmade and handwritten books of romance reflects a wide variety of original performance scenarios and a diversity of reading communities. The traditional story of the development and dissemination of romance is dominated by two well-known literary stereotypes of writing and reading, which are often depicted within romances themselves. On the one hand, there is the image of romance written and read within a courtly or aristocratic context, such as Criseyde reading the story of Thebes with a group of her ladies in Chaucer's *Troilus and Criseyde*. They are sitting in Criseyde's house in 'a paved parlour', a private, luxurious domestic setting, where 'a mayden reden hem the geste / Of the siege of Thebes, while hem leste' (II. 82; 83–4: a maiden read them the romance of the Siege of Thebes, while it pleased them). On the other hand, there is the image of romance being publicly recited or sung to an audience by a minstrel, at a feast or in an ale-house, such as the opening of the romance *Havelok*

Figure 24. The draft copy of the romance of *Sir Firumbras* is written on the back of documents relating to the dioceses of Exeter and Sherborne, dated 1357 and 1377. These were folded to form a protective envelope, within which the fair copy of the romance was then stored. Oxford, Bodleian Library, MS Ashmole 33 (2), binding fragments.

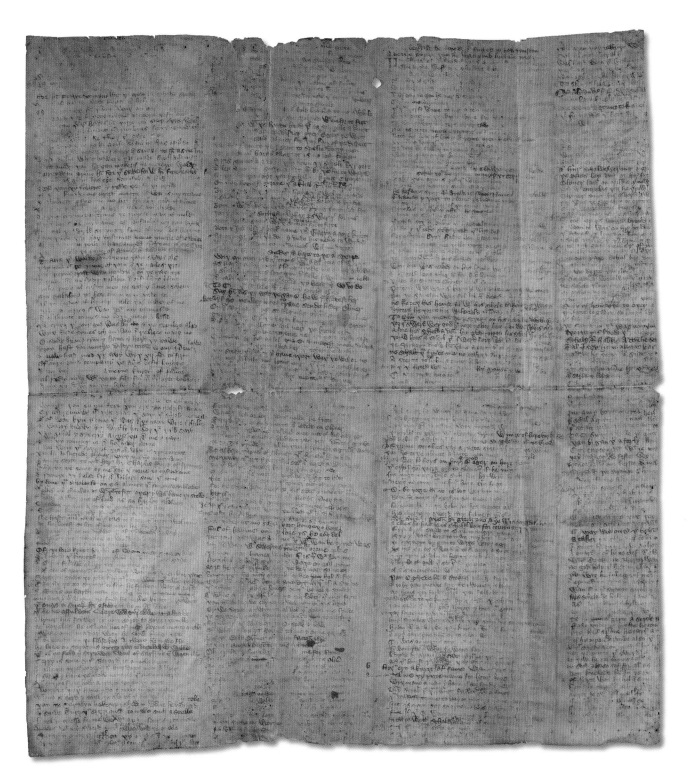

in which the narrator cries to his audience: 'At þe beginning of vre tale, / Fil me a cuppe of ful god ale; / And [y] wille drinken er y spelle' (lines 13–15: As we are now at the start of our story, fill up my cup with strong beer, so that I may drink as I speak).[1] These are points along the wide spectrum of romance reception in late medieval England. The modes and methods they portray certainly had a part to play in the story of romance reading. But to think of romance strictly in these stereotypical terms would be limiting and would belie a much more rich and varied history. The surviving handwritten medieval books are witnesses to a variety of communities within which romance was produced and consumed. They make it possible for us to locate romances within particular households and institutions: to eavesdrop on the original medieval worlds of romance.

The authors and translators of the majority of medieval verse romances are anonymous. However, there are occasional clues as to the identity of these individuals, such as the Bodleian Library copy of *Sir Firumbras*, from around

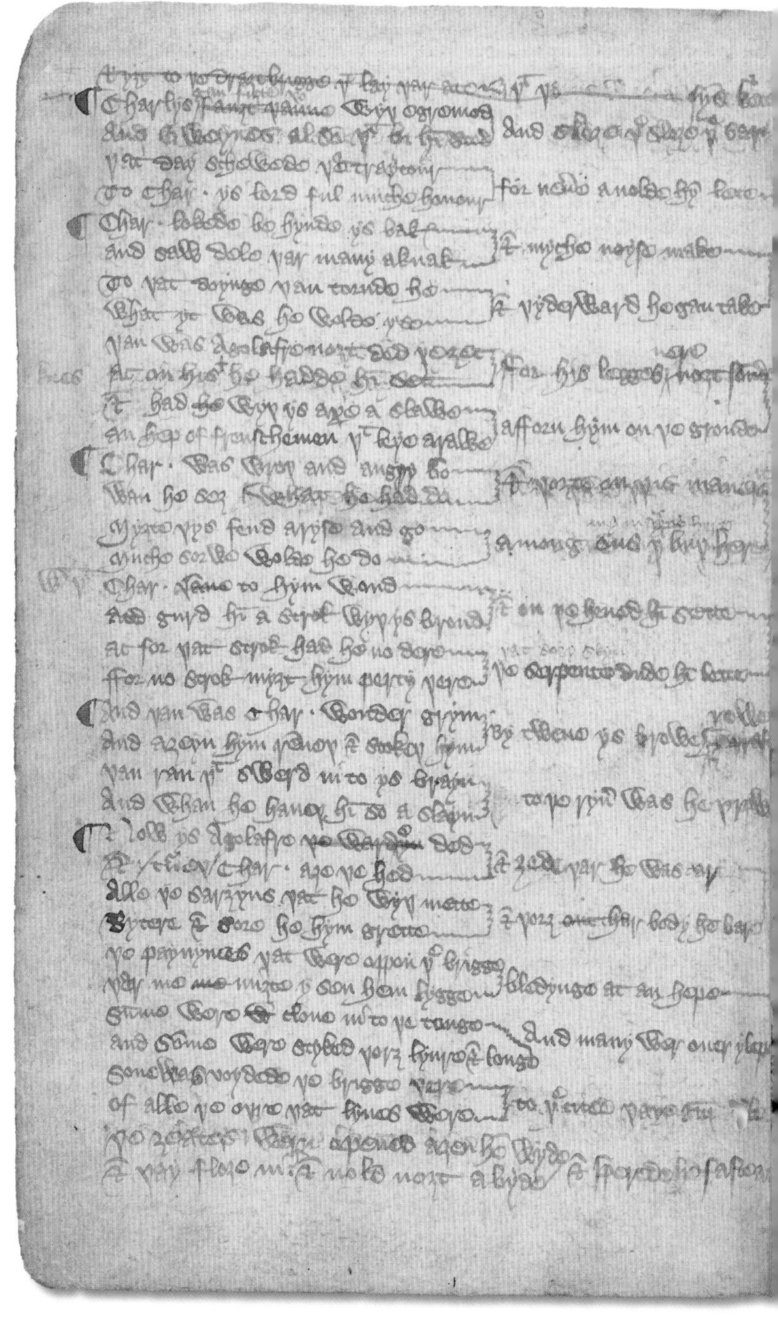

1380 (MS Ashmole 33). The story features the 'Saracen' knight Firumbras, who challenges Charlemagne's knights, is defeated by Oliver, and ultimately converts to Christianity. The Bodleian copy is remarkable because it contains not only the finished text of *Sir Firumbras* but also a rough draft with corrections (figs 24 and 25). The draft is written on the back of two large sheets of parchment that were folded twice to form a triple envelope and then used as a protective cover for the fair copy of the romance. It is extraordinarily rare to find an author's rough draft or autograph copy, not only among the Middle English romances but in English literature in general. It offers us an opportunity to observe romance composition in action: the numerous corrections in the draft illustrate how the romance was composed pen-in-hand and involved processes of careful correcting and rewriting. Thus, while oral memorization and spontaneous improvisation would have had a role to play in certain aspects of romance transmission, MS Ashmole 33 contributes to our understanding of more bookish and writerly methods. These methods would have applied to many of the romances that come down to us today which, like *Sir Firumbras*, are translations from Anglo-Norman, French or Latin, and stretch to several thousand lines.

We do not have a name for the composer of *Sir Firumbras*. However, various deductions can be made from the content of the thick parchment documents on which the rough draft is written – apparently the nearest thing to scrap note paper that came to hand. The documents are papal, which suggests the composer was a clergyman of some sort with access to such materials. The association of romance with clerical production should not seem

Figure 25. In addition to the rough draft, the composer of *Sir Firumbras* made numerous corrections to his romance. As can be seen here, there are many words in pen, in a paler ink but in the same hand as the main text, inserted above the line and in the margins. Oxford, Bodleian Library, MS Ashmole 33 (1), fol. 61v (south-west England, *c.* 1380).

surprising and there are other examples of the participation of the clergy and professional religious in the translation and composition of romances. A comparable case, and a near contemporary to the *Sir Firumbras* writer, is the scribe of the Bodleian's unique fragment of the Middle English romance *Apollonius of Tyre* (MS Douce 216). The fragment includes an inscription stating it was translated by one who refers to himself as 'vicary at wymborne mynstre'; that is, a vicar within the college of secular (non-monastic) canons at Wimborne Minster in Dorset. We can compare both these examples with the fictionalized representation of transmission in the French romance *Floire et Blancheflor*. The narrator begins with a description of how he overheard the story after dinner one evening: he listened as a group of sisters retired to a private room, where the elder of the women told the romance of Floire and Blancheflor, she herself having heard it from a clerk, who had read it from a book. That the originator of the romance is imagined to be a clerk suggests there was a traditional association between educated men – the clerical and literary intelligentsia – and the production of vernacular stories of romance.[2]

Both *Sir Firumbras* and *Apollonius of Tyre* exist only in these unique copies, so it is possible their circulation never extended very far. It may be that they were prepared for a particular event or patron. Both were written in the South West of England, from where the composers also seem to have originated: *Sir Firumbras* in Devon, in a dialect close to the dioceses of Exeter and Sherborne to which the papal documents relate; *Apollonius of Tyre* in Dorset, in a dialect close to the author's stated location at Wimborne Minster. That these two romances were of provincial origins is, in many senses, characteristic of fourteenth-century vernacular book production. Before 1400 London was not especially influential and London English no more prestigious than the English of other regions. As a result, literary compositions often came from the places where authors lived, in response to local cultural stimuli.[3] However, this is not to say by any means that authors always – or even usually – retained control over their romance texts, or that romances remained restricted to their original audience. As the depiction in *Floire et Blancheflor* suggests, romances had a tendency to glide between different modes and readers, and a clerically composed book of romance would not necessarily remain restricted to a clerical or male readership, or to the written mode. Once released from their earliest compositional circumstances, romances were regularly transformed and adapted by scribes or performers. Handwritten culture did not have the same notions of intellectual property, copyright or authorial ownership as modern print culture. The majority of romances are not, like *Sir Firumbras* and *Apollonius of Tyre*, written in the hand of their creator. On the contrary, the majority of those that come down to us today were copied many years after the original had been composed – transmitted either through writing, or through memory, or a combination of the two. A romance might therefore be re-copied in a new region and dialect, or adapted for a community with an entirely different set of needs and interests from those for which the romance was first created.

To illustrate the geographical and social movement of romance, it is worth considering the journey of *Richard Coeur de Lyon*, *Of Arthour and of Merlin* and *Kyng Alisaunder*. All three are from a single source: composed by the same London author around 1300.

All are lengthy (7–10,000 line) couplet romances that share features of form and style. *Richard Coeur de Lyon* recounts the exploits of King Richard I (1157–99) at the time of the Third Crusade and includes many historically precise details of the realities of war – such as equipment, geography and siege operations. Most notorious is its portrayal of Richard's demoniac personality and experiments with cannibalism, which involve feasting on Saracens' heads (as has been discussed in Chapter 2). *Of Arthour and of Merlin* traces the story of the youth of legendary British King Arthur through to his coronation and subsequent betrothal to Guinevere. It is interwoven with the story of Merlin's childhood, the development of his magical arts, and the role he played in Arthur's rise. *Kyng Alisaunder* recounts the story of Alexander the Great (356–23 BC) from his conception and birth, to the conquest of Darius, to his death, featuring details of his explorations in the east and the marvels he encountered there. Epic in scope and style and skilfully written, all three are distinguished by innovatory literary features such as the frequent lyrical passages on the theme of spring and the seasons, and the learned tone and vocabulary of the author, who often appeals to source-authority.

The earliest surviving copies of all three texts are found together in the same manuscript: the famous Auchinleck Manuscript (National Library of Scotland, Advocates' MS 19.2.1). Produced in London around 1340, this massive vellum volume would be regarded, by any standards, as an ambitious publication venture: of around 400 leaves, it contains over 44 texts, including 18 romances, and is distinguished by a visually attractive decorative scheme (fig. 26). This was a prestige purchase and represents a substantial investment of time and money. Its specific similarities with civic and royal books

Figure 26. This miniature appears at the head of the romance *Richard Coeur de Lyon* and features Richard and his army attacking by sea. It is one of very few images that survive in the famous Auchinleck Manuscript; many more were lost through vandalism: cut out as scrap-book trophies by a later collector. Edinburgh, National Library of Scotland, Advocates' MS 19.2.1, fol. 326ra (London, *c.* 1330–40).

for none
enin·
elknaun·
al ping·
bold·
g·
p tolde·
ing·
g & tolde·
bare·
nex· amen·

Lord [illegible] kyng of glorie
Whiche myght & whiche vertue
[illegible] kyng richard
[illegible] it is to here his stori
Of him to tell in [illegible]
[illegible] neuer no was coward·
[illegible] man [illegible] of [illegible]
[illegible] wreten what is in
[illegible] alamanie & [illegible]
[illegible] folk of fraunce·
[illegible] [illegible] in [illegible]
[illegible] duc of [illegible]·
[illegible] & of [illegible]
Of [illegible]
[illegible] & charlemain·
[illegible]
[illegible] ogeer·
[illegible]
[illegible] of [illegible]·
[illegible] no [illegible]
[illegible] also [illegible]·
[illegible] non·
[illegible] hundred [illegible] on·
[illegible]·
[illegible] gode [illegible]
[illegible] of [illegible]
[illegible] vnder stond·
[illegible] of ingland·

[illegible]
[illegible]
[illegible]
[illegible]
I no [illegible]
[illegible]
[illegible]
[illegible]
[illegible]
[illegible]
[illegible]
[illegible]
[illegible]
[illegible] ready [illegible]
[illegible]
[illegible]
[illegible] of fraunce [illegible]
[illegible]
[illegible] of [illegible]
[illegible] of [illegible]
[illegible] of [illegible]
[illegible]

implies it must have been intended for readers who operated at the very highest social levels – most likely from within the overlapping worlds of wealthy merchant traders, top-flight civil servants and high-ranking court counsellors. Moreover, there are many parallels and points of continuity between the texts in Auchinleck and the legal and historical documents and discourses through which the higher echelons of metropolitan society defined themselves and conducted business. In this context, the knowledgeable accounts of the realities of war found in *Richard Coeur de Lyon, Of Arthour and of Merlin* and *Kyng Alisaunder* would have offered test-beds for strategizing and decision-making; points of departure for debates about the legal and political implications of war and violence; sources for models of good and bad conduct during conflict; as well as examples of war-craft, international crusades and battle techniques. The marvellous, magical and entertaining aspects of these narratives (which are part of the reason we think of them as romances rather than histories) does not preclude their simultaneous use as sources for strategy and conduct. Rather, in this milieu, the book and its great heroes would provide serious models and precedents for members of the elite.[4]

Over the next century and a half the romances of *Richard Coeur de Lyon, Of Arthour and of Merlin* and *Kyng Alisaunder* were adapted and redeployed as they moved into different geographical regions and social circles. This included their appearance in far less lavish and expensive books than the prestigious Auchinleck Manuscript. There is the example of the Bodleian Library's single-text manuscript of a shortened version of *Richard Coeur de Lyon* from before 1500 (MS Douce 228; fig. 27). This modest paper pamphlet of just

Figure 27. The long, thin paper pages of this copy of *Richard Coeur de Lyon* have been heavily stained and worn through use and are now ragged at the edges. Oxford, Bodleian Library, MS Douce 228, fol. 1r (England, late fifteenth century).

41 leaves measuring 9 × 28 cm is written in a Norfolk dialect and we know, from the bookplate, that it was in Norfolk in 1736 when it was owned by 'Francis Blomefield, Rector of Fersfield in Norfolk'. The distinctive and highly dialectal colouration of the Norfolk language means that manuscripts that originated there are much less likely to have moved outside Norfolk while still in use, so it is possible it may always have circulated in this region.[5] A comparable example is the Bodleian Library's single-text manuscript of *Merlin* – a drastically shortened version of *Of Arthour and of Merlin* containing only the first part of the romance which relates Merlin's childhood antics and forms a humorous and entertaining prologue to the prolix, chronicle-style account of Arthour's life that follows in the full version (MS Douce 236; fig. 28). Copied from before 1500 into a Dorset dialect, its 37 vellum leaves measure just 12 × 16 cm: a genuine pocketbook production. Both MSS Douce 228 and 236 are flimsy unprepossessing books: easily stored and carried around, they were perhaps produced by scribe-owners for their own use. Their shortened texts, written in easy-to-follow single columns, suggest that reading aloud may well have been an important aspect of their intended function. It would be tempting to interpret the seventeenth-century ownership inscription in *Merlin* as evidence for ongoing shared use, circulation and reading aloud in the parish of Tolpuddle in Dorset: 'This is Robert Jones his booke recorde of Steven Jones and of Robert Webbe and of Misteris Caterne Jones and of many mo good people in the parishe of Tolpudle'. The inscription certainly reminds us that, however modest these books may appear, they were valued by early owners, and, though small in size, may have reached whole groups and communities of readers.

There are several more manuscripts in which these three romances are redeployed. There is the example of the fourteenth-century copy of *Kyng Alisaunder* in which Alexander's journeys around the Far East attracted attention as a kind of travel literature. This is indicated by the annotations of an early owner, who also added an account of 'Remarkable things and places seen in the pilgrimage of the Holy Land' (Bodleian Library MS Laud Misc. 622). Another example is the six-line lyrical description of spring from *Of Arthour and of Merlin*, which appears in a fifteenth-century manuscript without any acknowledgment and at the start of another romance entirely, *Orfeo*:

Mery tyme is in Aperelle,
That mekyll schewys of manys wylle.
In feldys and medewys flowrys spryng;
In grovys and wodys foules syng.
Than wex yong men jolyffe,
And than proudyth man and wyffe.

(lines 1–6, from Bodleian Library MS Ashmole 61, fol. 151r)

This kind of cut and paste between two otherwise apparently unrelated romances is typical of the flexible and unregulated culture of romance transmission. Rather than thinking of each romance as evolving in a linear progression, we should think of each existing as part of a network of developments and spin-offs. Compilers routinely customized the books they made,

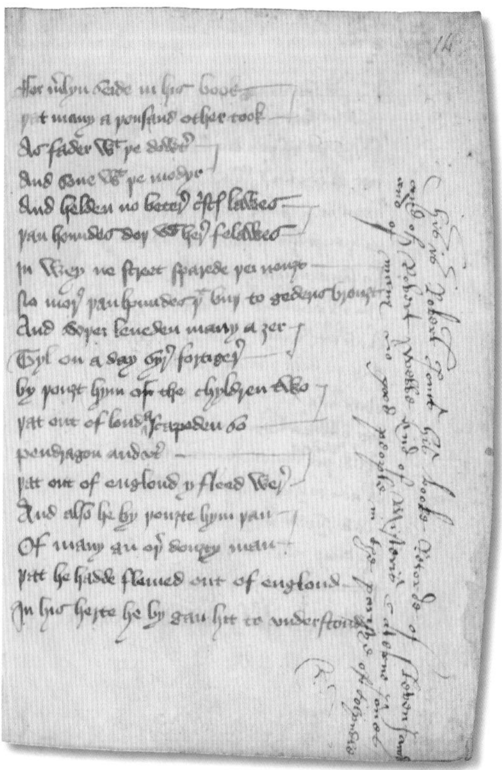

Figure 28. The tiny pocketbook which contains *Merlin* would have been easily carried around. The ownership inscription from the seventeenth century indicates that the book was in use for many years and was valued by these readers from Tolpuddle in Dorset. Oxford, Bodleian Library, MS Douce 236, fol. 14r (southern England, fifteenth century).

Figure 29. *pp. 74–5*. The massive and magnificent Vernon Manuscript, one of the largest books in the Bodleian Library, is likely to have been kept and read on a special desk or lectern. The homiletic romances it contains occupy only a very small fraction of its encyclopaedic compilation of spiritual verse from around 1390. Oxford, Bodleian Library MS Eng. poet. a. 1, fols 304v–305r (western England, *c.* 1390).

and often expressed a proprietorial attitude towards the anonymous verse romances they copied, adapting them and changing them, both linguistically and materially, to suit their own needs. In many ways, this aspect of informal book production has more in common with the unevenness, anonymity and responsiveness of web literature than with the apparent regularities and certainties of modern print culture: more fan fiction than Faber & Faber. As we have seen, within this unstable culture, *Richard Coeur de Lyon*, *Of Arthour and of Merlin* and *Kyng Alisaunder* were repeatedly adapted for different purposes – as works on war-craft, guidebooks for travellers, entertainment for reading aloud, or convenient sources to patch up missing sections of other texts – as well as being translated in and out of different dialects in an era where there was no single prestigious form of English. This tendency for individual romances to be radically altered and re-appropriated is one of the reasons for the wide variety of different kinds of manuscripts that can occur of a single romance.

The other reason for the wide variety of romance manuscripts is the elasticity of the romance genre itself. There are in the region of eighty different Middle English texts that could be classified as romances on the basis of their concerns with knighthood, chivalry and marvellous adventures. However, these eighty are very wide-ranging in terms of length, form, subject matter, tone and literary quality. For example, one group of 'romances' of notably pious theme have been justifiably classified within the subcategory of 'homiletic romance'. These include *The King of Tars*, *Robert of Sicily* and *Joseph of Arimathea*. In their form and mode of expression they have much in common with the romance genre. Yet, in each,

ȝif I schal touchen alle.
Þyn owne flesch. þe world. þe fend
Ac her þt schulde best. be þi frend
Þer þe þarest. to falle.
¶ And þat is þi flesch. þi furste fo
Þat þou þampuest and seruest so.
ȝif ich hit dorste seyen.
Þou dost þi soule. muche wrong
Whon þu makest. his fo so strong.
To fihten. him aȝeyn.
¶ Of þi furste fo. so fel.
Muche wonder. hit is to tel
Hose schulde. riht be synne
Þat such a foul stinkynde sek
Her such a burþen. in his nek
Of serwe. and of synne
¶ Þis caryen þt þu berest abouten
So ful wiþ inne. and wt outen
A lutel wormes mete.
Euer þe bet. þat þou hi do
Siker be þou. euer mo
Þe worse. he wol þe gete.
¶ And ȝif þu þenke. her uppon
Hou vyl a vessel. hit is on
ffor al þe metes. and drynkes
Hou hit schal foulore smelle & make
Þen eny caryene. þat is forsake
Of best. þat brere stinkes
¶ ffor hose bi heolde. þi bodi ariht
After þi der, a fourtenniht
Whore he þi frend. neuer so good
Þat he nolde hyȝen. him awey
And þynken seuen ȝer. of a day
Þat he. bi þe stod.

Þyn oþer fo. is a wonder þing
Þis world wt diuerse fondyng
Þenter þe. more & more.
ffals hit is. and fer hit semer
And whon hit aller best þe glemer
Hit greuer þe ful sore
Þis ffo. hab so a blendet þe.
Þat þu miht nouȝt. bifore þe se
Hou vyl þou art. and pore
Hou bare. in to þis world. þou come
Ne hou bare. þou wendest home
In to þi puttes ore
¶ He schewer þe wele & worldes wynne.
And diuers. so mony kinne
And asker þe. þer to
He ȝeuer þe. mony anibtes ȝeft
fforsake schuldestou. such a ȝeft
Þat þe con seruen so
¶ ffor whon þu hast gedred. al þi pride
Comer der. on þat oþer syde
And ȝeuer þe. al I. reue
And whon he hab. þe doun I. cast
He wol deceyuen þe. atte last
Ac hit. þin neuer neue
¶ Ac to þi put. he wol þe leden
And leue þe þere. wormes to feden
Loke which a seruise.
He seruer þe of & of no more
Þat al þi lyue. lustnest his lore
He quyter þe. on þis wyse
¶ And ȝit so schaltou. go þi wey
Naked and bare. weylawey.
Wrecche. hou hastou sped.
And ȝif þou haue. eny good wrouȝt
In word. in werk. or in þouȝt
Þat berest þou. to þi bed.

Vþridde fo. I may þe telle
Þt is þe foule fend of helle
Þe worste fo. of alle
Vnderstonde. he louer þe nouȝt
He wol changen al þi þouȝt
And maken þe. foule to falle
Vnderstonde. he wolde þe no good
He wolde marren al þi mood
Þow wer þe. from his hok.
And ȝif þou do. as I. þe seye

Al his wrenches. miht þou leye.
Al mid his owne crok
¶ ȝif þe fend. þorw his fondyng
Or for defaute. of wip stondyng
In eny synne. hab þe cast
Aris vp. as a Champioun
Stond stif. and fal no more adoun
ffor such a wyndes blast.
¶ Þow go. In to þe ferþe feld
And tak vr lord. to þi scheld
Þin hond. þou strecche and forde
And þenk uppon hi. wiþ myldo mod.
Þat for þe. ȝaf his herte blod.
And get þat lyflich. lorde
¶ Þow take þe crois. to þi staf
And þenk on hi. þat þer on ȝaf
His lyf. þat was so lef
Wite wel þi fot. wt stames old
And mak þe trayturr. speke þe word.
And wrek þe. on þat þef
¶ ffiht faste. for þyn owne riht
And get þe heuene. blisse briht
While þou hast tyme. þer to
Þin owne heritage. hit is
And þer of schaltou. neuer mis
But ȝif þou hit fordo.
¶ Ac ȝif þow haue wel in muynde
Hou feble. þat þou art of kuynde
And hou þou gost. to nouȝt.
Hit mihte wel þin herte whetten
And of ffleschles lustes. letten
Where þou wel. bi þouȝt
¶ Where ben heo. þat bi foren vs weren
Þat houndes ladden. & haukes beren
And hedden feld and wode.
Þis riche ladys. in heore bour
Þat wereden gold. in heore tressour
Wiþ heore brihte rode.
¶ Þei eten and dronken. & maden hem glad.
In Ioye was al heore lyf I. lad.
Men kneleden. hem bi foren.
Þei beren hem here. so stout and hyȝe
Ac in twynklyng of an eiȝe
Heore soules. weren forloren
Wher is þat gomen. and þat song
Þat trayling & þat comelich ȝong
Þo haukes. and þe houndes
Al þat Ioye. is went awey
Heore weole is comen. to welawei.
To monye harde. stoundes
¶ Heore paradys. þei hedden her
And now þei liggen. in helle fyr
Þer pit and peyne. is euere
Strong is þere. in peyne and wo
Ac hopen þay hem neuer mo
ffor out. ne comen þei neuere
¶ Allas þt þei euere weren boren or bred
Þat her on eorþe. such lyf han led
And deserued. such meedes.
To brenen. in þe fuir of helle
Euer more. þer inne to dwelle
And glowen in þo gledes.
¶ Ac moder & mayden. heuene aween
As we hopen. þat þou wol ben
Vr warant. from þe fende.
Þou help vs. dedly synne to fleen
And þat we mote. þi sone seen.
World wiþ outen ende. Amen.

Her bi ginner of þe kyng of Tars.
And of þe souda of Damas
Hou þe Soudan of Damas
Was cristned. þorw godes gras

Herkner now. boþe olde and ȝyng.
ffor marie loue þt swete þing.
Hou a werre bi gan.
Bi twene a god cristene kyng
And an heþene heih lordyng.
Of Damas. þe Soudan
Þe kyng of Tars. hedde a wyf.
Þe feireste. þat mihte bere lyf.

Þat eny mon. telle can.
A douȝter þei hadde. hem bitween.
Þat heore riht heir. scholde ben
Whit so feþer of swan.
¶ Chaast heo was. & fair of chere
Wiþ rode red. so blosme on brere
Eyen stepe. and gray
Lowe schuldres. & whit swere
Hire to seo. was gret preyere
Of princes þer. in play
¶ Þe word of hire. sprong ful wyde
ffer and ner. bi vche a syde.
Þe Soudan herde say.
Hi þouȝte his herte wolde breke on fiue
Bot he mihte haue hire to wyue
Þat was so feir a may.
¶ Þe Soudan. þer he sat in halle
He sente his messagers. faste wt alle
To hire fader. þe kyng.
And seide. hou so hit euer bi falle
Þat mayde he wolde. cloþe in palle
And spousen hire wiþ his ryng.
¶ And elles I. swere wt outen fayle
I. chul hire winnen in plein Batayle
Wiþ mony an heih lordyng.
Þe messagers. ben forþ I. went
To don heor lordes commaundement
Wiþ outen eny dwellyng.
¶ Whon þe kyng. þis vnderstood
ffor wraþþe neih. he wax wood.
And seyde. al in his talke.
Be hym þat dyȝed on þe Rod.
Rayer wolde I. spille my blod.
And in Batayle. ben slawe.
And al þe lond. þat is myn
Ar heo scholde wedde a Sarazyn
Þe deuel him er. to drawe
But heo wolle bi hire goode wille
Wende to hi. hire self to spille
Hire þouȝtes. nouht I. knawe
¶ Þat schul ȝe witen. ar ȝe pase
His douȝter to forþ. in þat place.
To fore hire fader blyue.
Douȝter he seide þe Soudan of Damas.
Desyrer. for to seo þi fas
And haue þe. to wyue
¶ Douȝter wost þu. for eny tresour
ffor sake crist. vr sauiour.
Þat soffrede woundes fyue
Þe mayde onswerde. wiþ mylde mood.
To hire ffader. þer he stod.
Nay lord. so mot I. þryue
¶ Ihesu þat dyȝed on þe tree
Let me neuere. þat day I. see
A tyraunt. for to take.
ffor marie loue. þat mayden free.
O. God and þsones þree
Bot ȝif hem wan. and wrake
¶ Douȝter he seide. beo now stille
Þow schalt neuer. be wedded hi tille
ffor bost þat he con make.
I schal him sende. such wordes to seyn.
Þat al his þouȝt. schal torne to veyn
ffor þou hast him forsake
¶ Bi þeos same messagers
Þat comen. from þe Soudan fers
Þeos wordes to him. he sent.
Heo nolde not leuen on his maners
To God heo made hire preyers
Þat lord. Omnipotent
¶ And bad him take. anoþer þouȝt
ffor hire ne scholde he wedde nouht
ffor gold. seluer. ne. rent
Whon þe messagers þis herde seyn
Soone þei torneden. hem aȝeyn
And to þe Soudan went
¶ Þe Soudan sat. at his des
I serued of his furste mes
Þei comen. In to þe halle
To fore þe prince. proud in pres.

Heore tale þei tolden wiþouten lees
And on heore knees gunne falle
And seide, Sire þe kyng of Tars
Of wikked wordes nis not scars,
Heþene hound he doþ þe calle;
And er his douhter he ȝiue þe tille,
Þin herte blod he wol spille
And þi Barouns alle.
Whon þe Soudan þis I-herde,
As a wod mon he ferde,
His Robe he rente adoun;
He tar þe her of hed and berd,
And seide he wolde hir winne wiþ swerd
Bi his lord seynt Mahoun.
Þe table adoun riht he smot
In to þe flore foot hot
He lokede as a wylde lyoun;
Al þat he hitte he smot doun riht
Boþe seriaunt and kniht,
Erl and eke Baroun.
So he ferde forsoþe a pliht
Al a day and al a niht
Þat no mon miht hym chaste;
A morwen whon hit was day liht
He sent his messagers ful riht
After his Barouns in haste.
Lordynges he seiþ, what to rede?
Me is don a gret misdede
Of Tars, þe cristene kyng;
I bed him boþe lond and lede
To haue his douhter in worli wede
And spouse hire wiþ my ryng;
And he seide wiþouten fayle
Furst he wolde me sle in Batayle
And mony a gret lordyng.
Ac certes he schal be forlore
Or to wroþerhele þat he was bore
Bote he hit þer to bring.
Þerfore lordinges I haue after ow sent
For to come to my parlement
To wite of ow counsayle.
And alle onswerde wiþ good entent
Þei wolde be at his comandement
Wiþouten eny fayle.
And whon þei were alle at his heste
Þe Soudan made a wel gret feste
For loue of his batayle.
Þe Soudan gedereþ an ost vnryde
Wiþ Sarazins of muchel pryde
Þe kyng of Tars to assayle.
Whon þe kyng hit herde þat tyde
He sente aboute on vche a syde
Alle þat he miȝte of seende;
Gret werre þo bigon to wake
For þe mariage ne moste be take
Of þat Mayden heende.
Batayle þei sette vppon a day
Wiþinne þe þridde day of May,
No lengor nolde þei leende.
Þe Soudan com wiþ gret power
Wiþ helm briht and feir baneer
Vppon þat kyng to wende.
Þe Soudan ladde an huge ost
And com wiþ muche pruide and bost
Wiþ þe kyng of Tars to fiȝte;
Wiþ hym mony a Sarazin feer,
Alle þe feldes feor and neer
Of helmes leomede lihte.
Þe kyng of Tars com also
Þe Soudan batayle for to do
Wiþ mony a cristene kniht;
Eiþer ost gon oþur assayle,
Þer bigon a strong Batayle
Þat grislych was of siht.
Þreo heþene aȝein twei cristene men
And felde hem doun in þe fen
Wiþ wepnes stif and goode;
Þe steorne Sarazins in þat fiht
Slowe vr cristene men doun riht,
Þei fouhte as heo weore woode.

¶ Þe Soudans ost in þat stounde
Feolde þe cristene to þe grounde,
Mony a freoly foode;
Þe Sarazins wiþouten fayle
Þe cristene culde in þat Batayle,
Was non þat hem wiþstode.
¶ Whon þe kyng of Tars saw þat siht
Wod he was for wraþþe a pliht;
In hond he hente a spere,
And to þe Soudan he rod ful riht,
Wiþ a dunt of muche miht
Adoun he gon him bere.
¶ Þe Soudan neiȝ he hedde islawe
But þritti þousent of heþene lawe
Coomen him for to were,
And brouȝten him aȝeyn vppon his stede,
And holpen him wel in þat nede
Þat no mon miȝte him dere.
¶ Whon he was brouht vppon his stede
He sprong as sparkle doþ of glede
For wraþþe and for envye;
Alle þat he hitte he made hem blede,
He ferde as he wolde awede,
Mahoun help he gan crye.
¶ Mony an helm þer was vnweved
And mony a Bacinet to-claved,
And sadeles mony emptye;
Men miȝte se vppon þe feld
Mony a kniht ded vnder scheld
Of þe cristene cumpaignye.
¶ Whon þe kyng of Tars saw hem so ryde
No lengor þer he nolde abyde,
Bote fleyh to his owne Cite;
Þe Sarazins þat ilke tyde
Slouȝ adoun bi vche a syde
Vr cristene folk so fre.
¶ Þe Sarazins þat tyme sauns fayle
Slowe vr cristene in Batayle,
Þat reuþe hit was to se;
And on þe morwe for heore sake
Truwes þei gunne to gidere take
A moneþ and dayes þre.
As þe kyng of Tars sat in his halle
He made ful gret deol wiþ alle
For þe folk þat he hedde I-lore;
His douhter com in riche palle,
On knees heo gon bi foren him falle
And seide wiþ syking sore:
¶ Fader heo seide, let me beo his wyf
Þat þer be no more strif
Þen haþ ben her bi fore.
For me haþ be muche folk schent,
Slawen and morþred and to-rent;
Allas þat I was bore.
¶ Fader, I chulle hit serue at wille
Erli and late, loude and stille,
And leeuen on God almiht;
Bote hit be so, he wol þe spille,
And al þi londes take hym tille
In Batayle and in fiht.
¶ Certes I nul no lengor dryue
Þat cristene men schul for me dye
Þoruȝ grace of God almiht.
Þen was þe kyng of Tars ful wo,
Anon he onswerde þo
To his douhter briht:
¶ Douhter he seide, blessed þou be
Of God þat sit in Trinite
Þe tyme þat þou were bore,
Þat þou wolt saue þi moder and me;
Þi preiere nou I graunte þe
Of þat þou hast bi fore.
¶ Fader heo seide, par charite,
And for Crist in Trinite
Blyne þat ich were þore,
Er eny more sorwe arere,
Þat ȝe ne my moder dere
For me beo nouȝt forlore.
¶ Þe kyng þo wiþ good entent
In to his chaumbre haþ I-sent

After his Qween so hende.
Whon heo was comen in present:
Dame he seide, vr douhter haþ ment
To þe Soudan for to wende.
¶ Dame he seide, counseyle me;
Her beoþ no mo bote we þre,
I-comen of cristene kende.
Þe Qween onswerde wiþouten fayle,
Þer to schal I neuere counsayle
Vre douhter for to schende.
¶ Þenne was þe douhter wo,
Mere heo quede hire moder þo
Wiþ a reuþful steuene:
Moder hit nis not longe a gon
Þat þer were for me slon
Þreo þousent men and seuene.
¶ And certes I nul no lengor dryue
Þat cristen men schul for me dye
Þoruȝ grace of God in heuene.
Weore þei wel, weore þei wroþe,
Þe douhter dude ouercome hem boþe
Bi riht reson and euene.
¶ Whon þei weoren þus at on
Messagers he sente anon
To þe proude Soudan,
To make frendes þat weore fon;
No mo folk þei wolde slon,
His douhter he graunted him þan.
¶ Whon þe messagers þus herde seyn
Smartliche þei torneden aȝeyn
To þe Soudan swart and wan.
Whon he herde heore lettres rad
Þen was he boþe bliþe and glad
And murie as eny man.
¶ And seide, I chul ben at his wille
Erly and late, loude and stille,
And help him at his neode;
No mo folk nul I nou spille.
Þe kyng anon he sende tille
And þonkede him of þat dede.
¶ Þe kyng and Qwene in chaumbre were þo
In care and sorwe and muche wo,
In stori as we rede;
Wel hem was wiþouten les
Þat þe Soudan wolde make pes
Wiþ cristen felawrede.
¶ Þis fel in a Somer tyde
Þe Soudan nolde no lengor byde,
To þe kyng of Tars he sent
Wiþ Sarazins and wiþ muche pryde,
Wiþ mony a Iuwel is nouȝt to hyde,
To make hym a present.
¶ Forþ þei went þat ilke tyde,
To þe kyng of Tars þei gan ryde,
Þat was boþe freo and gent.
Þei welcomed þe messagers;
Of gret reuþe ȝe may here
Whon þei to chaumbre went.
¶ In chaumbre kyng and Qwene was þo
In sorwe and care and muche wo
For heore douhter hende.
Heor douhter com bi fore hem wende
And bad hem bi hire counseil do
To saue cristene kende.
¶ Þe douhter þer wiþ wordes stille
Brouȝt hem boþe in beter wille,
And in to halle gunne wende,
And welcomede þe messagers
Þat come from þe Soudan fers
Wiþ wordes feire and hende.
¶ Þen seide þe Qwene after þan:
Hou fareþ ȝor lord þe Soudan
Þat is so noble a kniht?
Þe messagers onswere gan:
He fareþ as wel as eny man
And is ȝor frend a pliht.
¶ Þe Qween onswerde wiþ mylde mod
To þe messagers þer þei stod,
And seide þenne anon riht:
Ich fouche saaf on him my blod.

the features usually expected of a romance plot – a story of knightly prowess, chivalry and adventure – are either partly or wholly subordinated to hagiographical themes, moral topics and a religious mood and tone. As a result, all three are accommodated naturally into the Vernon Manuscript (Bodleian Library MS Eng. poet. a. 1): a compilation of unequivocally religious texts that was most likely produced by the Cistercians and intended for use within a religious community, perhaps a local nunnery (fig. 29). That is to say, the Vernon Manuscript was a book intended for spiritual instruction, and its romances were selected and read as moral exemplars and expressions of orthodox piety.[6]

Despite the similarities with saints' lives, not all medieval readers would necessarily have condoned the compiling of romance alongside texts of spiritual instruction in this way. One such individual is poet and ecclesiastical administrator William of Nassyngton (d.1354) – a secular cleric and establishment figure who outspokenly condemned romances for what he believed was their corrupting influence. So keen was Nassyngton to disassociate himself from a literary tradition based on love and chivalry that he defined his own literary work in terms of an opening declaration against romance: 'I will make no vayne karpyng of dedes of armes ne of amoures' (I will not vainly harp on about deeds of love and chivalry). His concerns reflect an era in which there was considerable anxiety over the use and availability of religious texts in English. We can certainly imagine that Nassyngton would not have approved of the compilation of his own text, the *Speculum vitae*, an erudite guide to good living, alongside a poem like *The King of Tars*, no matter how religious in tone it might be. Nevertheless, we must also observe

Figure 30. John Rate's name and drawings appear regularly in his home-made book, as can be seen here following the romance of *Sir Isumbras* and the 'Ten Commandments'. Oxford, Bodleian Library, MS Ashmole 61, fols 16v–17r (England (midlands), late fifteenth or early sixteenth century).

[...] ouer ye to wede
Sone the londes gon ye wyn
And stablyd cryston mor yerinne
In romanse as we rede
Than was the knyght Sir Isumbras
More better yan ever he was
And come of all his care
Iche of his sones he gaffe a lond
And corowned ye kyng wt hond
To lyue in myrthe evermore
They lyued & dyed wt god intent
And to heuen ye sawles went
When ye dede were

Amen quod Kate

(6)

Herkyns syrs wyth yt standes abowte
Of wyll zow tell wt gode entente
How ze to god schuld bow & lowte
Iff ze wyll kepe his comandment
Thow schall loff god wt herte entere
Wt all y soule And all y myght
Other god in no manere
Yu schall not haue be day ne nyght
Thy god name in vanyte
Thow schall not take for wolle ne wo
Remembyr the not yt o ye rode tree
For ye was made full blake & bloo
Thy holy daye kepe wele also
Fro wordly werk yu take y reste
All thy howsold ye same schall do
Bothe wyffe & chyld seruant & beste
Thy fader & moder yu schall honour
Not only wt thy reuerence
In all y nede be y socoure
And kepe aye godes obedience
Off mane kynd yu schall not sloy
Ne herme wt word ne wyll ne dede
Ne no mane gode yu take awey

Ne here yu make for frend ne foo
Kepe yu thy sawle full gretly aye
Thy neyzbors wyff yu nought desyre
Ne woman now thow schalt covet
But as holy chyrch wold it were
Ryght so ye purpose lyke yu sette
Hows ne lond ne oyr thing
Thow schall not covet wrongfully
But kepe well aye god byddyng
And ... forth kepe stedfastly
Ther be ye comandment X
yt were wryte in ye scrypture
That god gaff to moyses
Them to kepe late ze be sere
In two tabulles of ston ryght
To helpe mane kynd forth of synne
Wryten wt ye hond of god all myght
To teche man kynd ye wayes to wyne
All y that yes comandments kepe
In heuen wt god schall ever wone
Ziff yt they wyll he fynd them kepe
They schall be ... yer sone

Amen quod Kate

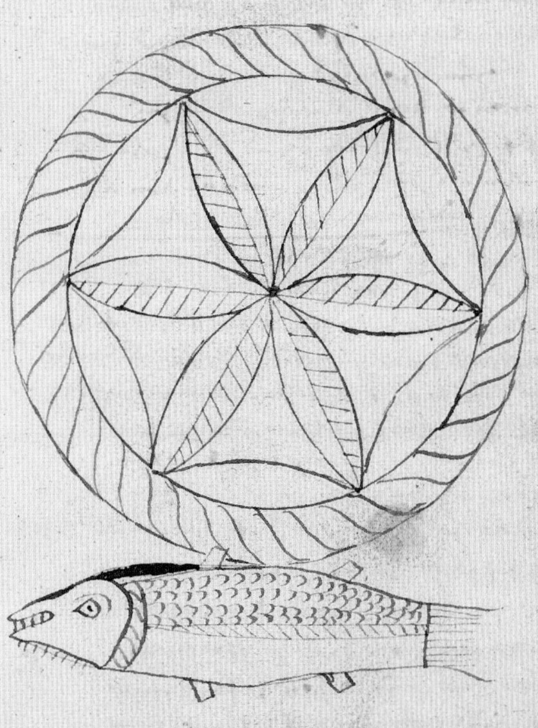

that the highly orthodox compilers of the Vernon Manuscript did not share these kinds of concerns, and both texts appear in their compendious volume. In fact, most medieval readers of romance seem to have had little compunction about gathering together romances with devotional materials and did not find incompatibilities there. On the contrary, many readers from the fifteenth century were keen to combine texts in exactly this way, including romances less obviously pious and religious than the ones selected for the Vernon Manuscript.

In this respect, we should consider the case of the book copied and compiled by a man called John Rate, who often signs his name in the volume (Bodleian Library MS Ashmole 61; fig. 30). Rate's book combines five romances – *Isumbras, The Earl of Toulouse, Lybeaus Desconus, Cleges* and *Orfeo* – with thirty-eight texts mainly of moral and spiritual instruction. Rate's decision to produce the book himself – he literally copied it in his own hand – would have allowed him full control over its contents and presentation. His remit seems to have been to gather together a selection of verse texts as a guidebook on how to live a pious and moral life within the framework of the family, such as could be read by or to the various members of his own household. The finished volume assembles texts that relate to many aspects of domestic life, including pragmatic and spiritual dimensions, and both light-hearted and serious topics. There are the poems of advice to the young 'How the Wise Man Taught His Son' and 'How the Good Wife Taught Her Daughter'; the stories of 'The Jealous Wife' and 'The Incestuous Daughter', which provide graphic explorations of destructive emotional and carnal forces threatening the family; a comic story about a cuckolded husband; saints' lives; practical guidance on the rules for purchasing land, healthy eating and table manners for children; and texts relating to the rhythms and routines of daily life, which include a prayer for the morning and a prayer for the evening. The romances underwrite this extremely conservative programme of reading and teaching and typically celebrate virtuous family life. So, *Isumbras* and *Cleges* both imagine the family as the setting for a happy life and end with the reunion of long-suffering families. And *Orfeo*, which presents Orfeo's retrieval of his wife Heurodis after her abduction by the fairies, may have been read as a commentary on emotional and psychological separation within marriage; or, indeed, as a commentary on wifely waywardness (fig. 31). The extent to which the actual readers complied with the models presented to them by Rate in his book remains in question. But the one thing Rate's selection of texts undoubtedly does imply is a perceived need to monitor and control domestic relations, not least disobedient wives and daughters.

Rate may have been a family chaplain, but more likely he was a merchant and head of the household. The Shield of the Passion drawing (fig. 32) that he added to his manuscript may relate to a merchant company in Leicester, which is also from where Rate's dialect originates. Certainly, the highly conservative programme of reading seems appropriate to such a figure: a city father and head of household concerned with the maintenance of law and order and with upholding traditional social roles and hierarchies. Further hints as to Rate's identity and the purpose of the book are implied by his additions throughout of pen-and-ink sketches of fish and stellate flowers (fig. 30). These show that Rate conceived of his

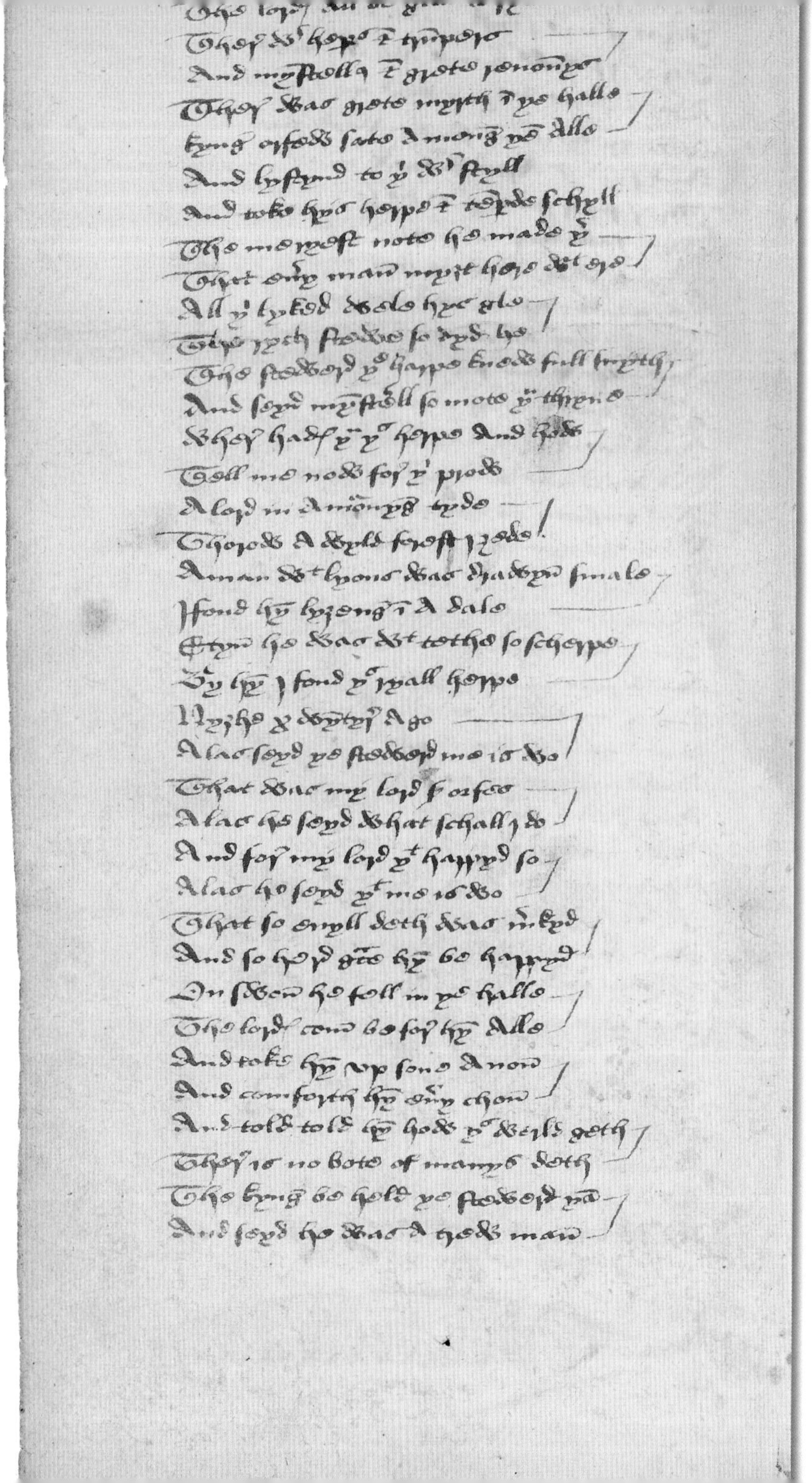

Figure 31. In this passage of *Orfeo* the loyal steward believes that Orfeo has been eaten by lions, and laments in a dramatic series of exclamations starting 'Alas'. This proves to Orfeo, disguised as a minstrel, that the steward is 'a trew man'. Oxford, Bodleian Library, MS Ashmole 61, fol. 155v.

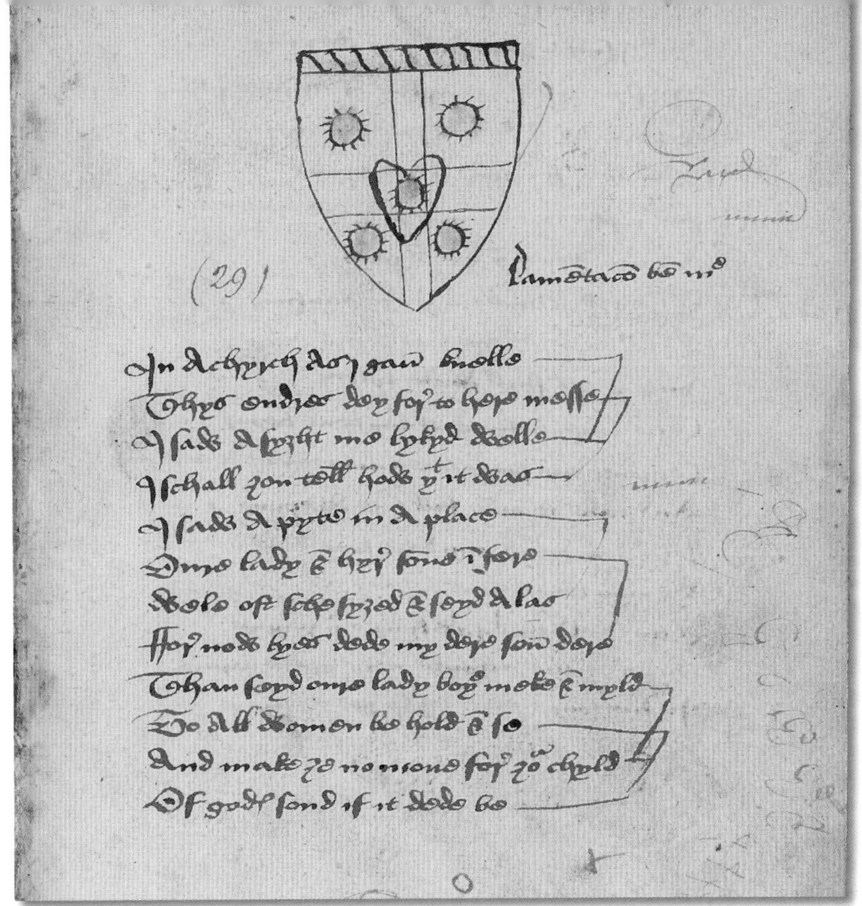

Figure 32. This drawing of the Shield of the Passion was added by John Rate before the 'Lamentacio Beate Marie'. Oxford, Bodleian Library, MS Ashmole 61, fol. 106r.

book as a coherent volume presenting a systematic programme of reading, not a casual collection of jottings. It may be that the fish and flowers represent the badge of Leicester's Corpus Christi Guild, which they resemble, and perhaps indicate that Rate was a member. Whether or not this is the case, they also send a very specific visual message to the book's users as they allude to the well-known ideas of 'gathering nectar from flowers of texts to furnish the cells of memory' and of 'fishing for remembered material in the trained memory'.[7] That is, Rate's fish and flowers seem designed to encourage readers to commit his book and its texts to memory: to develop their own internal crop of memorized lessons and exemplars that could be harvested to provide stores of daily moralistic wisdom. In this way Rate, through his book, attempts to delineate and define the collective identity of his household through a particular set of bourgeois values and brand of orthodox piety.

The examples of the Vernon Manuscript and of Rate's book show us some of the ways in which romance could appeal to those who were not intimately connected with matters of chivalry. However, this is not in any way to exclude other social groups from the readership of romance, such as those with more obvious vested interests in the values of the martial elite. We must remember that members of the gentry, in particular, were an important constituent of the readership of books of romance in the fifteenth century. The interrelationship between the gentry's political concerns and their interest in romance is visible, for example, in the book commissioned by Sir Thomas Hopton of Swillington near Leeds (Bodleian Library MS Digby 185). It has been described as 'a sort of family book', though it is one very different to Rate's pragmatic and unpretentious volume of bourgeois instruction and traditional tail-rhyme romance. By contrast, the Hopton book is an impressive, professionally produced volume, written on fine vellum in a high-grade (so-called Bastard Anglicana) calligraphic script. Most striking of all are the elaborately decorated coloured initials that appear at the start of each text (fig. 33). These incorporate the family's coats of arms and spell out, in heraldic form, their political loyalties and allegiances at a time when the men of the family were engaged in the military exploits of the Wars of the Roses. The book was perhaps intended for the Hopton sons and grandsons, as a commemorative object

Figure 33. The prestigious Hopton family book includes the romance of *King Ponthus and the Faire Sidone*, which opens with an elaborately decorated heraldic initial. Oxford, Bodleian Library, MS Digby 185, fol. 166r (England, mid-fifteenth century).

Now I wolle you tell a noble storye wherof a man may lerne many goode ensamples and yonge men may here the goode dedes of auncient people that dide muche goode and worship in theire days how it happened to the kyng Tiber of Spayne that kyng had to his wyf the kynges doghter of Aragon a full holy woman So thei had betwen theym a sonne that was called Ponthus the moste famose childe and the moste renowned that euer was seyn in that tyme The kyng his fader was a full worthy man and a stronge In that tyme it happened in the est that the Sawdyn of Babilon was of gret power of havyng men of armes So he had four sonnes wherthrugh he ordayned that the eldest shuld have his empire and sayd to the other thre after sonnes take ye noon hede to have any of myn heritage ffor I wolle ordeyn that eueryche of you shall have thirty m men of armes for the whiche I shal paye ther wages for the yer and shall gyve you shippyng and all that you nedes to have And eueryche of you thre shal goo in his aventur to conquer contrees and realmes upon the cristen and whiche of you thre that best doos and moste conquerys and moste enhaunces the lawe of Makomm shal be the best cherysed with me and I shal gyf to hym the moste of my goodes So the Sowdeyn ordayned his thre sonnes and praised theym that thei nede for to wer upon the cristen And thei went to the see all thre to gedre

So it happened as fortune wold that oon of the childer of the Sowdeyn come as the wynde drove hym and his navye by gret tormment that he passed Spayne in Galice and toke londe nygh to a gret citee that was called Couleigne and went to londe in a balyngers he and xxx men with hym and toke of the people ther aboute the londyng And when he asked who was lorde of that londe thei ansuerd and seyd that it was the realme of Spayne and that kyng Tiber was kyng of that londe Then asked the Sowdeyns sonne what lawe he held and thei ansuerd and seyd the lawe of Jhesu Criste Then made he to withdrawe his as though he wold withdrawe hym fro the contree And toke two and twenty shippes and sent theym to the porte of Couleigne and charged theyme to make theyme as merchandes of cloth of gold of silke and of spices and that thei shuld in the mornyng goo into the towne and logge theyme with forty men of armes with habyrgeons under ther gownes and in the morow erly that thei shuld come upon the walles at the water gate and that thei shuld kepe the gate And thei shuld assey to skale the wall and to come up into the towne And as thei devised it was so doon So come the xxij vessells and made theyme merchandes of spices and sold ther marchaundyse goode chepe and after that the forty men that were logged in the towne as marchaund nygh to the water gate thei made ther hostes to ete and drynk with theym that noon mysdoyng shuld be thoght And when thei had disported theyme thei went and had take ther avice to be up on the gate on the dawyng to goo aboute and devise ther doyng And when it come to the houre thei went upon the wall and at the same houre the sonne of the Sawdeyn that was called Brodas come to the foote of the wall with a grete and heirloom which would celebrate the family's chivalric heyday. This would certainly be compatible with the contents of the book, which includes the new, fashionable, prose romance of *King Ponthus and the Faire Sidone*: a version of the Horn legend, translated into Middle English prose in the early fifteenth century from a French adaptation. The emphasis in *King Ponthus and the Faire Sidone* on conduct and the rules of proper behaviour for gentlemen, combined with its themes of loyalty, particularly political loyalty, would have made it suitable for the instruction of the sons of the household. Further lessons in gentlemanly conduct could have been provided by the copy of Hoccleve's *The Regiment of Princes*, and in political loyalty by the book's other major text, the historical chronicle known as the *Brut*. To finish off the young men's instruction, Hoccleve's tale of Jonathas warns of the duplicities of women.[8]

The books of Rate and Hopton each express and define the distinctive interests and concerns of their households. Both could be described, in their own ways, as being dominated by the markedly masculine perspectives of their compiler or commissioner. Yet both may well have been used by female readers in the context of the household. These women – like the female religious community for whom the Vernon Manuscript may have been intended – remain shadowy figures. Typically women are less visible in the historical record, yet we must not underestimate their importance in the transmission of romance. There is a literary tradition of associating women with romance reading. The examples of Criseyde and her women, and the sisters reading *Floire et Blancheflor*, have been discussed at the start of this chapter, but there are others. There is the description in *Reinbrun* of the accomplishments of an

African princess, which include 'romaunce reding'.[9] Of less exalted social status is the girl in a lyric 'The Fair Maid of Ribblesdale' (in London, British Library Harley MS 2253), whose attractive mouth and lips ('mury mouht' and 'lefly rede leppes lele') are imagined as ideal for reading romances ('romaunz forte rede').[10] And Chaucer playfully points to women as the primary readers of romance in *The Nun's Priest's Tale* where he refers to the 'booke of Launcelot de Lake, / That wommen holde in greet reverence'.[11] Frustratingly, there are no names of female readers inscribed in books of romance before 1500, although this does not mean they did not own or use these books. Confirmation comes from occasional external references to actual women readers and owners, such as the copy of the romance *Partonope of Blois* given by Isabel Lyston in her will in 1490/1 to her daughter Margery London, along with 'my best rynge of gold such as sche will chese' and 'myn englyssh boke of saynt margarets lyfe'. It is an exchange which shows us how books could pass through the female line, and which suggests the appeal of *Partonope of Blois* to women – a romance in which the narrator explicitly addresses women, and whose heroine, Melior, displays an exceptional degree of agency, autonomy and power in the tale. We may wonder whether Isabel and Margery's *Partonope of Blois* is one of the three medieval copies now held by the Bodleian Library, two of which are fragmentary, though with no ownership inscription it is not possible to be sure (fig. 34).[12]

The examples discussed in this chapter show us how medieval romance underwent continual material and literary transformations that were unregulated and were in response to the rich cultural context of medieval England. The culture and technology of reading and writing medieval romance was radically creative, open, dynamic and unstable. There were myriad functions of romance within medieval culture, which is partly a reflection of the diversity of different romances, which deal with all sorts of themes, topics, locations and events, and are written in a variety of forms and modes. But it is also a reflection of the way that a single romance could, itself, be adapted for a range of purposes and environments. Examination of actual books and readers shows to us their dispersal around the country in different regions, across the social spectrum, and in relation to various communities and settings. This tendency for romances to be altered and appropriated is part of the elusive nature of the romance genre, as well as the reason for its success and persistence through centuries of cultural change. The surviving manuscripts provide us with pieces of this complex and dazzling mosaic. They remind us that each handwritten copy of romance was the locus for a sequence of unique medieval events involving scribes, compilers, owners, readers and listeners.[13]

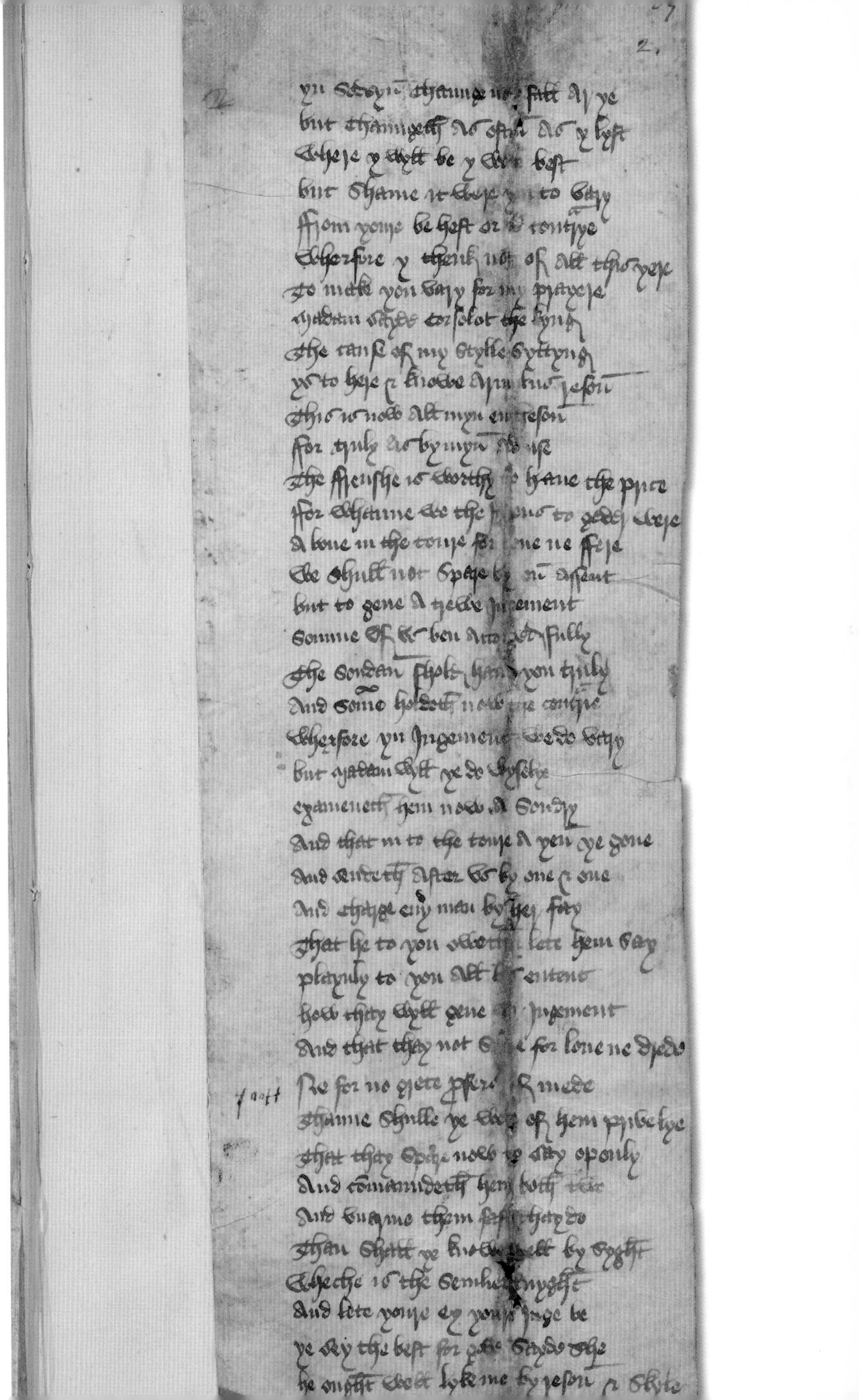

Figure 34. *Partonope of Blois* derives from a twelfth-century French romance of love and magic, *Partonopeu de Blois*; its fifteenth-century English translator also took inspiration from Chaucer's narrative style. This copy was originally written in two columns, but now only two much-damaged leaves remain. Oxford, Bodleian Library, MS Eng. poet. c. 3, fol. 7r (England, fifteenth century).

seigniorie z, de droit par rayson, si que il va la disme de toutes les choses qui viennent les nefs se prennent de nel de marchandises soutilles, par sentenar, et de pourveoit bien, et de lanigna le sel, et du sandal, et des autres marchandises, x. par sentenar, il y a de toutes choses de vivre en grant habondance. Et sachiez que pres de ceste cite de [illegible], si a une autre cite qui a anon tinugui la ou se fait moult de voilles de porcelainnes qui sont moult belles, car autre part ne se font fors en ceste cite. Et aves son vent [illegible] aillors et si en a len grant marchie. Car pour i. gros venicien en auroit on en auroit bien iii. des communaument les plus belles que len pourroit trouver. Et de ceste cite se portent par tout le monde. Il ont en ceste cite [illegible] i. autre langage par eulz. Or vous ai conte de ce royaume de tinguy que len appelle [illegible] une partie quinte est de ceste part si est si comme autre fois vous avons dit la neufvisme partie de la [illegible] du mangy. Et vous di que le grant caan en a bien si grant droit, et si grans rentes de ce dit royaume de tinoncha, et plus grant encore que il na du royaume de quin[illegible]. Or vous avons conte de tous les royaumes de mangy et de quinsay, et de fugui, et de tanguy nauons nous pas encore dit de ce auez vous bien entendu. des autres vi. royaumes. Nous saurions bien conter, mais pour ce que ce est trop longue matiere si nous en tairons a tant. Et vous avez moult tres bien entendu tout le fait du cathay et du mangy et de toutes autres provinces si come nostre livre le vous conte trestout apertement et par droit ordre, et lun apres lautre. Et tout ce vous avons nous dit sans faillir. Et ainsi ques vous avons nous dit des manieres le[illegible] uns. Et aussi des manieres de toutes les au

Chapter 4

Nicholas Perkins

Dangerous Encounters

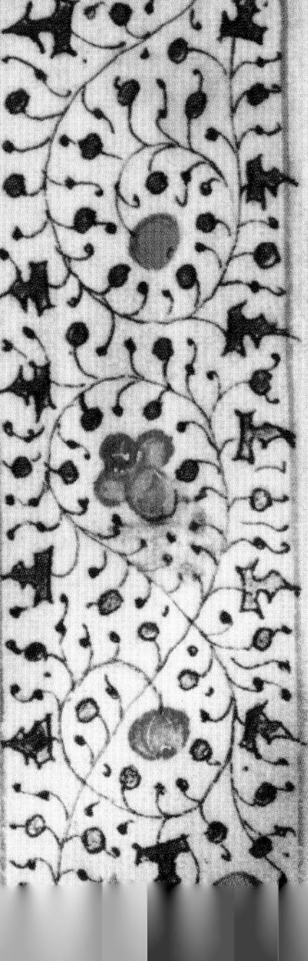

We have seen how varied are the traces that romances leave in books and other cultural forms throughout the Middle Ages. Sometimes they appear in institutional productions, as with *The King of Tars* and *Robert of Sicily* in the Vernon Manuscript, encouraging their use as tools for teaching religious and ethical lessons. Other romances engage with Christian belief more personally and unpredictably. In *Isumbras,* an angel asks the hero to choose whether to endure suffering early or late in life (he picks the former). In *Amis and Amiloun,* the bond of blood-brotherhood between the eponymous protagonists threatens all other relationships, leading to perjury, leprosy and child-killing, with voices from heaven intervening to warn or explain. *Gowther* also employs Church institutions to generate shock or resolve a narrative impasse. Gowther is conceived when his mother has sex under a tree with a demon masquerading as her husband; their child's diabolical behaviour includes tearing the nipple from his mother's breast and burning nuns. The Pope later begins Gowther's rehabilitation by requiring him to scavenge for scraps left by his host's dogs. He eventually becomes a worthy knight and emperor, building an abbey to replace the one he had destroyed.[1]

Figure 35. The Tristan tiles, found at the site of Chertsey Abbey, Surrey, are among the finest surviving medieval tiles. Here Tristan, disguised as a pilgrim, climbs aboard Iseult's boat. While carrying her ashore he deliberately tumbles to the ground with her, so that Iseult can swear truthfully that she has had no one between her legs except her husband King Mark, and the pilgrim. British Museum, AN 17518001 (England, *c.* 1260–70). © Trustees of the British Museum.

Romances could have more than an imagined connection with ecclesiastical buildings too: they were embedded in the fabric of medieval churches, through motifs on misericords, gargoyles and roof bosses, and emerge, for example, in the 'relics' connected to King Arthur proudly hosted by Glastonbury Abbey. Another abbey – Chertsey, in Surrey – had magnificent thirteenth-century floor tiles, including depictions of Richard the Lionheart and Saladin, and Tristan and Iseult, probably acquired through the abbey's royal patronage (fig. 35).[2] This latter narrative of illicit desire seems an extreme case of accommodating romance in religious institutions, unless the Chertsey monks could read the story inventively as a morality tale. Such crossovers are characteristic of the long reach of romance into many areas of medieval life, but the waywardness of romance, especially its ability to define itself against authoritative texts and institutions, also generated friction. In Chaucer's *Canterbury Tales*, when the Host invites the Parson to continue their story-telling game, he receives short shrift:

Thou getest fable noon ytolde for me, *no fiction told by me*
For Paul, that writeth unto Thymothee,
Repreveth hem that weyven soothfastnesse *those who ignore truthfulness*
And tellen fables and swich wreccednesse. (X. 31–4)

The Parson's Tale is a prose treatise warning against the seven deadly sins. Pride, envy, anger, avarice, greed, lust and sloth all find fertile soil in the romances and other fables that the Canterbury pilgrims hear, and medieval depictions of lovers often hover ambivalently between virtuous restraint and the tug of physical desire (fig. 36).

Figure 36. An ivory mirror back depicts two lovers in an embrace. Their animal passion is suggested by the squirrel on the lady's arm, and the horse held in check by his groom – a motif also familiar from illustrations of the Adoration of the Magi. In the background, a female attendant plays a rebec. Ivory-carved mirrors, combs and *gravoirs* (hair parters) were often owned as a set, their imagery frequently playing on themes of desire and service. © Ashmolean Museum, University of Oxford. WA 2001.178 (Paris, first half of fourteenth century).

Perhaps the most famous account of the dangers of romance reading, itself framed as a captivating love story, appears in Dante's *Divine Comedy* (*c.*1308–21). In Canto V of *Inferno*, Dante's alter ego and his guide, the poet Virgil, meet Francesca di Rimini, whose doomed affair with her husband's brother Paolo has condemned them to drift in the second circle of hell, along with Dido, Helen, Paris, Achilles and others. Francesca relates how reading of Lancelot and Guinevere sealed their own fate:

> Per più fiate li occhi ci sospinse
> quella lettura, e scolorocci il viso;
> ma solo un punto fu quell che ci vines.
> Quando leggemmo il disiato riso
> esser basciato da cotanto amante,
> questi, che mai da me non fia diviso,
> la bocca mi basciò tutto tremante.
> Galeotto fu 'l libro e chi lo scrisse:
> quell giorno più no vi leggemmo avante.[3]
>
> [Several times that reading urged our eyes to meet and drained the colour from our faces; but one moment alone overcame us. When we read how the longed-for smile was kissed by so great a lover, this one – who shall never be parted from me – kissed my mouth all trembling. A Gallehault [*go-between, pander*] was the book and he who wrote it; that day we read no farther in it.]

In this extraordinary scene, the romance of Lancelot itself becomes the catalyst for the lovers' kiss, actively urging eyes and mouths to respond to its erotic power. Bodleian MS Holkham misc. 48 (fig. 37) illustrates this passage of *Inferno* with the pained souls drifting at the mercy of their 'dubbiosi disiri' (V. 120: dubious [*or* dangerous] desires).

Figure 37. Here in Dante's *Inferno*, Dante and Virgil see the drifting souls of those enslaved by desire in the second circle of Hell, including Tristan, and on the right Paolo and Francesca forever bound together. Oxford, Bodleian Library, MS Holkham misc. 48, p. 8 (Northern Italy, *c.* 1350–1375).

These souls include Tristan, whose love for Iseult exemplifies how romance treats desire as dangerous intoxication. Tristan and Iseult unwittingly drink the love potion intended for Iseult and King Mark, Tristan's lord, and tumble into a love that tears at the heart of the court. Their story is retold in dozens of versions throughout the Middle Ages, including Gottfried von Strasbourg's brilliant *Tristan* in German (whose narrative lies behind Wagner's opera); the Old Norse *Tristrams saga ok Ísöndar*; and the Middle English *Tristrem* in the Auchinleck Manuscript, in which Hudain the dog also laps up the lovers' potion and is besotted with them. As the Chertsey tiles demonstrate, the story was widely disseminated in visual media too (fig. 38).[4] One of the earliest extant written versions is the fragmentary *Tristan* of Thomas of Britain, composed *c.*1160, which Gottfried acknowledges as his major source (Bodleian MS Fr. d. 16: fig. 39). Tristan's brilliant accomplishments in hunting, conversation, music and poetry, along with his military prowess, contribute to a performance of desirable masculinity for the twelfth-century courtly and aspirational audience. Yet these accomplishments contrast vividly with the blows that fortune deals to the lovers. It is often said that the literature of this period forges the meaning of romantic love for Western European culture. Here in Thomas's poem, love is grafted to pain, absence and sickness; desire is a teasing and unquenchable force; and sexual union is also the splitting of the self:

Ysolt en sa chambre suspire
Pur Tristan que tant desire,
Ne puet en sun cuer el penser
Fors ço sulment: Tristan amer;
Ele nen ad alter voleir

Figure 38. This striking wooden casket retains some of its original paint. Its lid depicts the famous scene of Tristan and Iseult under a tree in which King Mark has hidden to eavesdrop on them. Seeing his reflection in a pool, they avoid incriminating themselves, and here Mark is shown with a sword, attacking the dwarf who informed him about the assignation. Victoria and Albert Museum, 2173-1855 (possibly the Netherlands, *c.* 1350–70). Photo © Victoria and Albert Museum, London.

Figure 39. This manuscript contains fragments of the *Tristan* of Thomas of Britain. The picture has sustained some damage, but Tristan is characteristically depicted harping, demonstrating his prowess in courtly as well as military accomplishments, and his connections with arts of poetry and song. Oxford, Bodleian Library, MS Fr. d. 16, fol. 10r (England or France, late twelfth or early thirteenth century).

Ne alter amur, ne alter espeir,
En lui est trestuit nun desir,
E ne puet rien de lui oïr.[5]

[In her chamber, Queen Ysolt sighs for Tristan, whom she desires so much. She cannot think about anything in her heart except this alone: loving Tristan. She has no other wish or love, no other hope. All her desire is on him, and yet she can hear no news of him.]

The Tristan story keys directly into debates over the art and practice of love in the twelfth and thirteenth centuries, which have often been associated with the Angevin court of Henry II and Eleanor of Aquitaine, and with Eleanor's daughter Marie de Champagne, cited as a patron by Chrétien de Troyes in his *Lancelot*. While the catch-all term 'courtly love' is now viewed with scepticism by scholars, many romances are certainly impelled by the minute investigation of human desire, with the etiquette, rhetoric and private imaginings that accompany it. The Anglo-Norman *Folie Tristan d'Oxford* (named thus because this version survives only in Bodleian MS Douce d. 6) takes one shard of the Tristan narrative and allows it to refract many aspects of the dangerous play of love. Tristan is desperate to see Iseult, and hatches a plan to infiltrate King Mark's court:

Pur vostre amur sui afolez,
si sui venu, e nel savez ...
feindre mei fol e faire folie,
dunc n'est ço sen e grant veisdie?[6]

[I've gone mad for your love, yet I'm here and you don't know it ... I'll pretend I'm a fool, behave as if mad. Isn't that clever and a stroke of cunning?]

In Mark's hearing, he calls himself 'Tantris' and declares that he loves Iseult. He retells details of their liaisons, but the shocking truth is treated as delusion. Later, in Iseult's chamber, Tantris the ugly lunatic cannot convince her that he really is Tristan, even when their dog Husdent recognizes him and runs up, 'bute del vis, fert del pé' (rubbing him with his muzzle, patting him with his paws).[7] Only when Tristan speaks in his own voice does Iseult believe him. The madness of love here rivals any insanity, while the faithful lover is also a traitor to the king. These contraries unsettle the widespread use of romance to give models of virtuous behaviour and ideal courtship, as in the fine frontispiece illustration of a loving couple in Bodleian MS Ashmole 45, and *The Earl of Toulouse* that follows, with its story of a virtuous wife resisting attempts on her honour (figs 55–57).

The madness of desire and loss surfaces in many romances, which literalize the emotional metaphors that we still live by. In *Orfeo*, the hero's wife Heurodis (Meroudys in Bodleian MS Ashmole 61) sleeps under an 'hympe-tre' (line 58) and has a dream foretelling her abduction:

Sche cryed, and grete noys gan make,	*noise*
And wrong hyr hondys with drery mode,	*doleful state*
And crachyd hyr visage all on blode ...	*scratched her face*
And was ravysed out of hyr wytte.[8]	*taken out of her mind*

Despite the protection of Orfeo's army, she is snatched away to the fairy kingdom. Orfeo leaves his court to live 'wyth wyld bestys euer-mor' (line 220), mad with grief. As with Tristan, so Orfeo eventually uses his musical skills to his advantage. He travels to

Figure 40. This small enamelled case displays scenes perhaps from a lost romance, *Sir Enyas and the Wodewose*. On this side, Enyas delivers runs through a *wodewose* (wildman) who brandishes a club and heart-shaped shield. The case may have been designed to contain a tiny book, and hang from a girdle. Victoria and Albert Museum, 218-1874 (England or France, *c.* 1325). Photo © Victoria and Albert Museum, London.

the fairy Otherworld, where bodies of the taken are displayed in suspended animation, some grotesquely mutilated. Disguised as a minstrel, he extracts a rash promise from the Fairy King that Orfeo can name his prize after harping so exquisitely. He claims his wife, and they escape this realm of fear, or death. Drawing deeply on folk legend as well as classical sources, *Orfeo* is one of the texts copied by a scribe named Rate in Bodleian MS Ashmole 61 (see pp. 78–82). Its positioning there amid moral and religious material, including texts on the deadly sins and vanity, might encourage us to speculate on the symbolic significance of Orfeo's journey, as many Christian readers of the Orpheus legend did. Rate titles the poem 'Kyng Orfew', and it could also yield instruction on keeping promises, dealing with adversaries and managing a royal household. Orfeo is fortunate that the steward in whose hands he leaves his kingdom acts well, relinquishing authority back to his lord; many romance heroes are not so lucky.

The story of Yvain combines some dark motifs with comedy and a debate over identities both human and animal. In the Welsh version from The Red Book of Hergest (fig. 19), Owein tells his wife that he will accompany Arthur to Britain for three months. However, he forgets her and stays for three years. When a maiden arrives to retrieve his wife's ring and condemn his desertion, he breaks down and heads for the mountains: 'Ac ef a vu y velly ar dro hyny daruu y dillat oll, ac hyny daruu y gorff hayach, ac yny dyuawd blew hir trwydyaw oll' (And he wandered about like this until all his clothes disintegrated and his body all but gave out and long hair grew all over him). One day some ladies find him. They look him over and even feel him: 'Sef y gwelynt gwytheu yn llamu arnaw'

(They could see his veins throbbing).[9] One maiden is instructed to rub a little medicinal ointment onto this shaggy but intriguing creature. She ends up using the whole jar, and Owein comes to his senses, realizing that he is naked. This episode enjoys vicariously gazing at and massaging a bare male body, and probes the boundary between wildman and human, nature and culture. Later, Owein rescues a lion from a serpent; the lion becomes his companion and lieutenant, much to the disgruntlement of Owein's opponents, who point out the unfairness of having to fight both man and beast. The lion gives the story comic impetus, but also projects Owein's growing sense of self, his ability to make the right ethical choices and eventually regain both his wife and his place at Arthur's court.

Romances frequently use these techniques of projection and boundary-testing to challenge their audience's understanding of human desires and motivation. The doppelgänger, the fairy mistress, the flesh-eating giant and the fire-breathing dragon all perform this repertoire of the monstrous and uncanny, whose excess helps us to understand our own wants. An exquisite enamelled case now in the Victoria and Albert Museum depicts scenes probably from *Sir Enyas and the Wodewose*, a romance whose text is lost but whose story can be reconstructed from carvings and manuscript pictures (fig. 40). Having saved a lady from a *wodewose* (wildman), Enyas is jilted by her in favour of a younger knight, who then challenges Eynas for ownership of his (more loyal) dog. Enyas kills him and leaves the ungrateful lady in the forest, to be devoured by wild beasts. In *Eglamour*, the hero fights giants, a boar and a dragon (fig. 41), but the narrative connects these projections of excessive masculinity to Eglamour's prospective father-in-law, who tries to frustrate the

Figure 41. Eglamour encounters a huge boar, whose previous victims' remains lie scattered on the ground. Later he fights a giant who kept this boar as a pet, and laments the death of '[m]y lytyll spotted hogelynne'. Oxford, Bodleian Library, MS Douce 261, fol. 32v (England, 1564).

He ſawe the bore come from the Sea
Hys mornynges draught had he tane
The boore ſawe where the knyght ſtode
Hys tuſkes he whetted as he were wode
To hym he drewe that tyme
Syr Eglamoure wened well to do
With a ſpeare he rode hym to
As faſte as he myght renne
All yf he rode neuer ſo faſte
The good ſpeare a ſonder braſte.

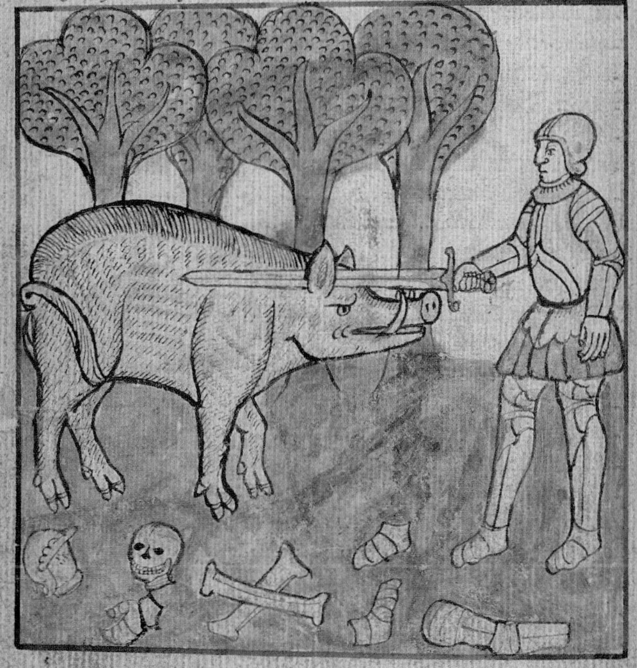

It woulde not in the hyde
That boore dyd hym wo ynoughe
Hys good horſe vnder hym he ſloughe
On foote than muſte he byde
Eglamoure ſawe no boote that tyde
But to an oke he ſett hys ſyde
Amonge the greate trees thore
Hys good ſwerde he drewe out than
And ſmotte vpon the wyllde ſwyne
Two dayes and ſomedele more
Tyll the thyrde daye at noone
Eglamoure thought hys lyfe was done
For feyghtynge with that boore
Than Eglamoure withe eger mode
Smotte on the boores headde
Hys tuſkes he ſmote of there
The kinge of Satyn on huntynge dyd fare
With fyftye armed men and more
The boore loude herde he yell
He commaunded a ſquyer to fare
Some man ys in peryll there
I trowe to longe we dwell
No longer wolde the ſquyer tary
But thyder rode faſt by Saynt mary
He was thereto full ſnell
Vppe to the Clyffe rode he thore
Syr Eglamoure fought faſt with the bore
With ſtrokes fyers and fell
The Squyer ſtode and behelde them two
He wente agayne and tolde ſoo
For ſothe the boore ys ſlayne
Lorde, Saynt Mary howe may thys be

young lovers' desires. The motif of father–daughter incest is deeply set in many romances, and forms the fulcrum of the Apollonius legend. In *Eglamour,* the Oedipal father must be defeated before the next generation can flourish. The analogous figure of threat in the haunting Scottish romance *Eger and Grime* (included in the Percy Folio: see pp. 137–8) is the mysterious Graysteel, who guards a forbidden land. Eger is left for dead by Graysteel, who takes a gruesome token from each of his victims: their little finger. While Eger convalesces, his sworn brother Grime masquerades as him to avenge the defeat and restore Eger's manly reputation. Grime kills Graysteel:

> & againe to the dead body he yeede, *went*
> & pulled forth his Noble Brand,
> & smote of Sir Gray steeles hande:
> 'My brother left a fingar in this land with thee,
> therefore thy whole hand shall he see.'[10]

In a grimly comic moment, Grime later hands a glove to the lady whose family Graysteel has terrorized, and who nursed Eger through his wounds. When she takes it, out falls Graysteel's bloody hand. As with Dante's description of a book commanding eyes and lips to do its bidding, the Green Knight's gory head, or Lancelot's fetishistic devotion to a lock of Guinevere's hair, in *Eger and Grime* the anatomy of fear and desire is animated by the sometimes severed body parts of its protagonists.

These mythic and symbolic landscapes work in symbiosis with traditions of exploration and discovery, including the encounters with other peoples or religions that we described in Chapter 2.

Figure 42. A French account of Marco Polo's voyages is illustrated with monstrous races: creatures such as the Blemmyae, with heads beneath their shoulders; Sciopods with one leg; and the dog-headed Cynocephalus. Oxford, Bodleian Library, MS Bodl. 264, fol. 260r (England, early fifteenth century).

[illegible] chapitre le commencement
du livre dynde. et devisera toutes les merveilles
qui y sont et les manieres des gens.

Or puis que vous avez oy conter
de tantes provinces de terre nous
vous laisserons de ceste matiere
si vous commencerons a entrer
en ynde por vous conter toutes
les merveilles qui y sont. Si commencerons pre-
mierement de leur nez en quoi li marchant vont

World maps such as the Hereford Mappa Mundi include depictions of the so-called monstrous races, lurking around the biblical or historical events and places at the map's conceptual centre.[11] Alexander the Great is particularly associated with these imaginative geographies, and the Hereford map depicts some of his exploits. In Bodleian Library, MS Bodl. 264, along with the Alexander texts' own fascination with the exotic, the manuscript's English adaptors added *Li Livres du graunt Caam*, a French version of Marco Polo's travels, drawing together the genres of romance and exploration, and including pictures that mingle finely drawn detail, old traditions of the marginal races, and deformed beings crowding the manuscript's own margins (fig. 42).

The poet of *Sir Gawain and the Green Knight* teases us by glossing over Gawain's encounters with such dangerous beasts and 'wodwos' in the 'wyldrenesse of Wyrale' (lines 721, 701) as Gawain seeks the Green Knight. Instead, the foul English weather bothers him most. Gawain finally encounters a castle so perfect it seems cut from paper. His glamorous hosts there are Bertilak and his wife. Having promised to exchange any winnings the two men gain, Bertilak sets out hunting while Gawain stays in bed and finds Bertilak's wife offering far more hospitality than the virtuous knight finds comfortable:

> ȝe schal not rise of your bedde. I rych yow better:
> I schal happe yow here þat other half als,
> And syþen karp wyth my knyȝt þat I kaȝt haue. (lines 1223–5)

[You shan't get out of bed. I have a better idea: I shall tuck you up on the other side too, and then talk with my knight, whom I've captured.]

Figure 43. Lady Bertilak stands over Gawain while he pretends to sleep, chucking him under the chin. Above the picture is a rhyming motto added to the manuscript that reflects on love and loyalty. London, British Library, MS Cotton Nero A. x, fol. 129r © British Library Board (England, *c.* 1400).

Figure 44. A bronze aquamanile (water vessel) depicts the story of Phyllis riding Aristotle. Annoyed that the philosopher had advised Alexander against his distracting infatuation for Phyllis his wife, she provokes Aristotle to fall for her, and demands that she ride him like a horse, telling Alexander where he can witness this strange reversal. The story pokes fun at the old philosopher, but also warns of the dangers of allowing desire to overcome reason. Phyllis's dangling girdle prominently emphasizes her dominant sexuality (Netherlands, *c.* 1400). © 2011. Image copyright The Metropolitan Museum of Art/ Art Resource/Scala, Florence.

This scene is illustrated in British Library MS Cotton Nero A.x (fig. 43). The lady's fashionably loose sleeve points at Gawain's body – naked under the covers – as if pinning him down, while she provocatively tickles him under the chin, alone in the curtained bed. Gawain feigns sleep, but must soon defend his virtue in a battle of wits more dangerously flirtatious than any Cary Grant movie – part of a playful repertoire of medieval narratives imagining women on top (fig. 44). Each day, Gawain exchanges the mounting number of kisses he receives from his host's wife for the beasts that Bertilak has killed. Hovering over these scenes is the prospect of Gawain having to exchange something more intimate with Bertilak if he succumbs to the Lady's invitations. On the final day, Gawain kisses Bertilak three times, but hides an apparently magic protective girdle that the Lady has given him. Of course, we soon discover that the mysterious Green Knight and the jovial Bertilak are one and the same, and that his wife deliberately tempted Gawain to breach his most important knightly quality of *trawþe* (truth, loyalty, faith). The Green Knight cuts Gawain on the neck to remind him of his slip, and his rueful arrival at Arthur's court provokes a debate over whether he deserves praise or, as Gawain feels, blame.

The *Gawain*-Poet's brilliant play with our expectations about ethics and romance has singled this poem out for generations of readers and adaptors, but Gawain frequently appears in late Middle English romances, whether as Arthur's troubleshooter or as a figure whose womanizing reputation is ripe for comic development. The fifteenth-century *Wedding of Sir Gawain and Dame Ragnelle* combines these elements. As in the *Awntyrs off Arthur*, Arthur has unjustly taken lands from a knight, Sir Gromer Somer Jour, who surprises the king unarmed. To escape death, Arthur must discover what women most desire. He enlists Gawain's help, and they fill a book with possible answers. Eventually the king encounters an ugly hag who promises to help. The answer is not beauty, sex or flattery, she assures him:

> We desyren of men above alle maner thing *more than anything else*
> To have the sovereynté, withoute lesyng, *authority; lying*
> Of alle, bothe hyghe and lowe.[12]

Her price for saving Arthur is marrying Gawain, and the poem lavishes description on her boorish manners and bad teeth at the wedding feast. Once married, she challenges the famously courteous Gawain to '[s]hewe me your cortesy in bed' (line 630). Ragnelle then offers Gawain a choice: she can be attractive by day and ugly by night, or vice versa. By allowing her to decide, he breaks an enchantment and gains a permanently beautiful wife. The 'loathly lady' motif is used in several romances, including Chaucer's The Wife of Bath's Tale, to engage both comedy and debate around female desires, authority and the mistake of judging by appearances. It is familiar to a new generation of romance viewers (with a politically correct twist) in the film *Shrek*, where Princess Fiona becomes a full-time ogress by kissing her monster-hero. The only surviving copy of *The Wedding of Sir Gawain and Dame Ragnelle* is Bodleian MS Rawl. C.86 (fig. 54). It consists of several originally separate sections, which mingle religious, historical and moral texts, medicinal recipes, scurrilous verses, and other tales, including *Landeval*. Also included are two Canterbury tales – those of the Clerk and the Prioress – and *The Legend of Dido*, from Chaucer's *The Legend*

Figure 45. The opening of Chaucer's *Troilus and Criseyde*. This folio was added to the manuscript after the main text was initially copied. The God of Love casts an arrow, while Troilus and Criseyde (labelled in gold on their waists) look across at one another. This fine manuscript is now stored unbound after previous bindings have trimmed the pages, creating a series of separate leaves rather than gatherings of folios. Oxford, Bodleian Library, MS Arch. Selden B. 24, fol. 1r (Scotland, soon after 1488).

The double sorowe of Troylus to tellen
That was the kinge Priamus sone of Troye
In lovinge how his aventures befellen
From wo to wele and after out of Joye
My purpos is or that I parte ʒow froye
Thesiphone thou help me for tendyte
Thes wofull vers that wepinge as I wryte

To the clepe I thou goddess of turment
Thou cruell furye sorowinge ever in peyne
Help me that am the sorowfull instrument
That helpeth loveres as I can compleyne
For wele sitt it the sothe for to seyne
A wofull wight to have a drery fere
And to a sorowfull tale a sory chere

For I that God of loves servantes serve
Ne dare to love for myn unlikelynesse
Preyen for spede all schold I therfor sterve
So fer am I from his help in derknesse
But nathelees if this may don gladnesse
Unto any lover and his cause availle
Have he my thank and myn be this travaille

But ye loveres that bathen in gladnesse
If any drope of pitee in ʒow be ʒow
Remembreth ʒow on passed hevynesse
That ye have felt and on the adversite
Of other folke and thinketh how that ye
Have felt that love durst ʒou displese
Or ye have wonne him with to grete an ese

And preyeth for theme that bene in the cas
Of Troilus as ye may after here
That love theme bringe in hevene to solas
And also for me preyeth to God so dere
That I have myght to schewe in som manere
Swich peyne and wo as loveres folk endure
In Troylus unsely aventure

of Good Women. The manuscript's concentration of stories about or using the voice of women, and its mingling of the practical, devotional and obscene, make this a fascinating document of late fifteenth- and sixteenth-century reading practice.[13]

In the Prologue to *The Legend of Good Women*, Chaucer dramatizes the dangers of a hostile audience for the writer of romance. He meets the God of Love in a dream, who threatens him with death for giving women a bad reputation, for example in his poem *Troilus and Criseyde*. In fact, Chaucer's unsummarizable masterpiece about love, faith, destiny and loss provides an intensely subtle exploration of human desire, its dangers and rewards. When Troilus first sees Criseyde in besieged, doomed Troy, his previously scornful attitude to love is overthrown by the God of Love, whose vengeful arrow of desire strikes Troilus. In turn, Troilus's glance across a crowded temple is imagined as a missile:

> And upon cas bifel that thorugh a route — *it chanced that through a crowd*
> His eye percede, and so depe it wente, — *pierced*
> Til on Criseyde it smot, and ther it stente. — *struck; stopped*
> (I. 271–3)

Criseyde's look back at him kindles a burning desire, and he suffers the pains of love longing (fig. 45). Through the many thousand lines of its intricate plot, *Troilus and Criseyde* traces the progress of this secret relationship, through its climax in Book III as the two make love in a small upstairs chamber (fig. 46), to Criseyde's being sent to the Greek camp in a prisoner exchange and infamously breaking a promise to return. As Troilus discovers, human existence itself is akin to being a prisoner, awaiting the judgement of capricious gods. Contrary to the God of Love's misreading in *The Legend of Good*

Figure 46. Troilus and Criseyde kiss and go to bed, from Pierre de Beauveau's *Roman de Troÿle*. The candle in each scene signals the flaming passion of the lovers. Oxford, Bodleian Library, MS Douce 331, fol. 26r (France, c. 1450–1475).

auoit si grant sommeil
quelle ne se pouoit plus
soustenir Apres ce que
chun fut couche et lostel

sir et lattendant prest et appareille
de luy obeyr comme seruiteur
doit faire a sa dame mais
tresse et amie

La belle tenoit
vng flambeau
en la main et

toute seulle descendit les
degrez et vit troyle qui
lattendoit Lequel elle salua

faillir tant est sage et
discret se par aucune mal
le fortune nestoit · dont dieu
le gard et de ma part je

ment a conduire son fait
par facon et si bonne ma
niere quil vous plaira
Et adieu soyes

Parti que fut pan
dare · sen ala la
belle briseyda
toute seullette en sa chabre
en son cueur chinne parole

quelle mesmes deuise en
ceste maniere En souspi
rant souventesfois et
pensant en troyle plus
quelle navoit acoustume

Women, Chaucer does not allow the misogynist tradition of fickle Criseyde to go unchallenged. He explores the web of constraints under which she must operate, as a widow, a traitor's daughter, an object in exchanges between men. Pandarus, her uncle and Troilus's confidant, is central to these exchanges; his emotional blackmail and vicarious pleasure in the lovers' union have become a byword for the unctuousness of the courtier and fixer (fig. 47).[14] Despite all this, Criseyde remains a thinking subject, whose path to love is traced in intimate detail, and who later predicts (and thus challenges) her future reputation.

In the famously ambivalent ending of *Troilus and Criseyde*, Troilus's spirit ascends to the eighth celestial sphere and laughs at human folly, before the poem's voice stridently condemns the whole enterprise of pagan, worldly love. No less ambivalent in its treatment of the fleshly and spiritual is the baggy collection of Arthurian romances that trace the quest for the Holy Grail, expanding massively the treatment of this myth in Chrétien de Troyes' *Perceval*. This Vulgate Cycle (or *Lancelot–Grail* Cycle) was developed in thirteenth-century France. Its porous texture of interlaced stories allowed for numerous further continuations, stretching the boundaries of romance narrative to breaking point. The Cycle reaches back to site the Grail's origins in biblical narrative, fleshes out the adulterous love between Lancelot and Guinevere, and follows the questing knights as they encounter demonic temptresses and wandering dwarfs, moments of spiritual insight, moralizing hermits, and one another in disguise (fig. 48). It is only the virgin knight Galahad who fully accomplishes the Grail quest; others are held back through sin. This highly charged spiritual quest, laden with magical objects,

Figure 47. Pandarus talks to Criseyde at a window. The conversational scene and sober clothing of Criseyde, a widow, is placed in counterpoint to the sinister, suggestive actions of the monkey and dog in the foreground. Oxford, Bodleian Library, MS Douce 331, fol. 15r (France, *c.* 1450–1475).

relics and prophecies, attempts to align codes of Christian knighthood with the energy of romance narrative. It then folds the Grail story into the death of Arthur and downfall of the Round Table, linking the court's moral failings with its destruction. However, as Caxton acknowledges in his edition of Malory's *Le Morte Darthur* (see p. 16), the dangerous pleasures of romance are never far from the didactic material, and many of the Cycle's readers must surely have let the moralizing pass them by and simply enjoyed the tales of glinting weapons, inadvisable sex and bloody violence, often richly illustrated as in Bodleian MS Rawlinson Q. b. 6 (fig. 49). Malory's great synthesis of Arthurian romances pares back the Grail story to focus on moments of individual insight and revelation, but the darkening tone of Malory's narrative as it heads towards Arthur's death is set by this tension between spiritual ideals and the tug of worldly desires. As Sir Ector says over Lancelot's corpse, in a speech laden with the irresistible contradictions of Malory's and many other romances:

> [T]hou were the curtest [*most courteous*] knyght that ever bare shelde! And thou were the truest frende to thy lovar that ever bestrade hors, and thou were the trewest lover, of a sinful man, that ever loved woman, and thou were the kindest man that ever strake wyth swerde.[15]

Figure 48. Lancelot approaches a lady in bed, from the *Lancelot–Grail* romance cycle. In this episode, the lady objects to an exhausted Lancelot resting there, as she is unchaperoned. Oxford, Bodleian Library, MS Douce 199, fol. 221v (France, *c.* 1325–1350).

lenuit en son chemin & chevalcha par les forie
es tant quil vint pres de kamaalot · De ce aue
ture qui li avenist puis quil se parti de corbenic
ne parole lestoire fors qui a la cort de pentecoste
lamanie · Si lesse ore li contes a parler de lui & re
torne a lancelot

Or Dit li contes que quant lanc · se fu
partis de lvoys il chevalcha a droit vers
la lumiere quil veoit com cil q' mestier
avoit de herbergier · car asses avoit este
ce iour las & travelliez & quant il vint

Figure 49. A large illustrated copy of parts of the *Lancelot–Grail* Cycle, finishing with the *Mort Artu*. One of its scribes names himself as Ernoul d'Amiens. The text is punctuated by miniatures that highlight the drama of the action, but also help a reader navigate around a long and complex series of narratives. Oxford, Bodleian Library, MS Rawl. Q. b. 6, fol. 136r (northern France, early fourteenth century).

The miniatures shown here are: fol. 136r (Gawain is captured and attacked with flails); fol. 160r (Lancelot risks humiliation by riding on a cart to pursue Guinevere's captors); fol. 211r (Guinevere, thinking Lancelot is dead, laments in his chamber); fol. 346v (Galahad with the red cross shield, whose history is traced back to Josephus, son of Joseph of Arimathea. Spenser's Redcrosse Knight in *The Faerie Queene* owes much to Galahad, as well as the cross of Saint George).

philosophye that he knewe the science of thynges to come here after/he saide to me many tymes and affermed for trouthe/That yf parys your sone wente in to grece for to take ony noble lady by vyolence/ That this noble cyte shold be destroyed and brente in to asshes by the grekes and that ye and alle yowris shold be slayn cruelly/And therfore ryght sage and wyse kynge plese hit your noblesse to here my worde and beleue that the wyse men haue sayd/ And also in that thynge that ye may not lese to leue/ And wherof grete sorowe may ensiewe yf ye perseuere / wherfore wyll ye put an enbusshement vpon your reste/ And to put your tranquyllite vnder the dangerouses auentures of fortune / Leue this and departe yow yf hit plese yow fro this folye / And parfyne and ende your lyf in reste eurousely/ And suffre not parys to goo in to grece in Armes And yf ye wolle algate Sende ye another than parys / At these wordes of pantheus sourded and aroose grete murmures of the herers/ Some reprouyd the prophecyes of deufrobe the philosopher/ And some helde hit for mocquerye and fable / And they were of the grettest nombre / in so moche that by the consente of the more partye/ Parys was compysed for to go in to grece wyth men of Armes / And the parlament fynysshid eche man wente hym home in to his hous and to his place .

Whan this conclusion was comen to the knowleche of cassandra the doughter of kynge pryant / she began to make so grete sorowe / As she had be folysshe or oute of her mynde . And began to crye an hyghe sayng .

Chapter 5

Alison Wiggins

Romance in the Age of Print

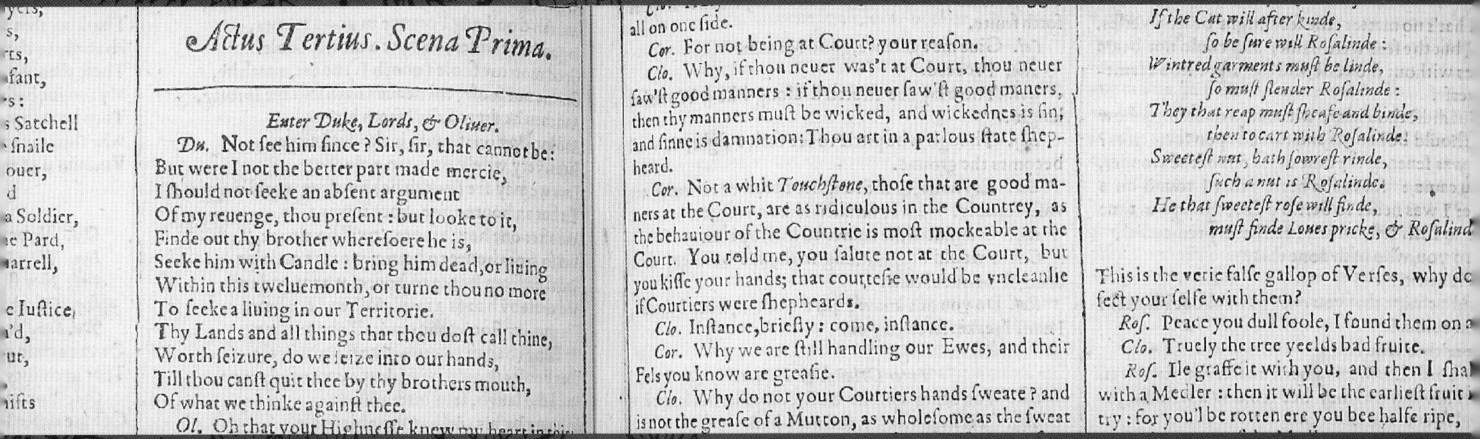

THE END of the Middle Ages was not the end of medieval romance. Tudor and Elizabethan readers and writers engaged with the literary tradition of native romance and the result was a range of lively and creative responses. Many of the structures and motifs of traditional romance persisted, but they were adjusted, repackaged and reconfigured in response to the expectations and perceptions of new readers. Romance thus continued to have a vibrant life in the midst of enormous cultural, political, religious and technological change. As medieval romance endured it was reshaped by the pressures of new milieux and by contact with radically different kinds of romance – from the fantastical worlds of Ludovico Ariosto's *Orlando furioso* (first published 1516, with a more complete text appearing in 1532) to the best-selling multi-volume *Amadis of Gaul* (first published in 1508 and translated into many languages), and from the reimagining of pastoral in Philip Sidney's *Arcadia* (*c.*1580) to the brilliant parody of romance in Miguel de Cervantes's *Don Quixote* (1605, Volume I; 1615, Volume II; fig. 50). Old and new versions of romance interacted and were interspersed with one another during the early years of printing right through to the final plays of Shakespeare. In this way, the period itself is given shape by the versions and transformations of romance that

Figure 50. *Don Quixote* affectionately mocks the excesses of romance through its protagonist Alonso Quixano, who falls into madness by reading old chivalric stories and takes up the life of a knight errant, dubbing himself Don Quixote de la Mancha. Thomas Shelton's translation was the first in English, this edition being produced in 1620 by Edward Blount, who was also involved in publishing the first folio edition of Shakespeare's plays. Oxford, Bodleian Library, 4° L 32(2) Art., title page.

THE
HISTORY OF
DON-QVICHOTE.
The first parte.
PRINTED FOR ED: BLOUNTE
BODLEIAN.

more than nyne ſkore and ten yere / And was ſo wyſe in philoſophye that he knewe the ſcience of thynges to come here after / he ſaide to me many tymes and affermed for trouthe / That yf parys your ſone wente in to grece for to take ony noble lady by vyolence / That this noble cyte ſhold be deſtroyed and brente in to aſſhes by the grekes and that ye and alle yowris ſhold be ſlayn cruelly / And therfore ryght ſage and wyſe kynge pleſe hit your nobleſſe to here my worde and beleue that the wyſe men haue ſayd / And alſo in that thynge that ye may not leſe to leue / And wherof grete ſorowe may enſewe yf ye perſeuere / wherfore wyll ye put an enbuſſhement vpon your reſte / And to put your tranquyllite vnder the dangereuſes auentures of fortune / Leue this and departe yow yf hit pleſe yow fro this folye / And parfyne and ende your lyf in reſte ewreuſly / And ſuffre not parys to goo in to grece in Armes And yf ye wolle algate Sende ye another than parys / At theſe wordes of pantheus ſourded and arooſe grete murmures of the herers / Some reprouyd the prophecyes of deufrobe the philoſopher / And ſome helde hit for mocquerye and fable / And they were of the grettest nombre / in ſo moche that by the conſente of the more partye / Parys was compyſed for to go in to grece wyth men of Armes / And the parlament fynyſſhid eche man wente hym home in to his hous and to his place .

Whan this concluſion was comen to the knowleche of caſſandra the doughter of kynge pryant / ſhe began to make ſo grete ſorowe / As ſhe had be folyſſh or oute of her mynde . And began to crye an hyghe ſayng .

mark its boundaries. The first book to be printed in English was a romance: *The Recuyell of the Historyes of Troye*, newly translated from French into English and printed by William Caxton in Bruges *c.*1473 (fig. 51).[1] Fresh to the English market, it reflects Caxton's interest in publishing courtly, chivalric translations of fashionable continental prose romances designed to appeal to an aristocratic clientele. When Caxton's successor Wynkyn de Worde took over the business in 1492, he to some extent followed Caxton's policy of issuing successful continental works. But these were augmented with the kind of traditional verse romances that had been avoided by Caxton, familiar favourites such as *Guy of Warwick*, *Bevis of Hamtoun*, *Eglamour of Artois* and *Degaré*. The choices of England's first two printers reflect, then, in miniature, the alternations and negotiations between traditional romance and new imports that recur throughout the era.

The top-selling titles of Tudor England tended to be practical and instructive works, but there was still a vigorous demand for romance judging by the number and variety of prints and reprints. Romance represented a viable publication venture due to a pre-existing market, based on its earlier wide dissemination. Over eighty different romances are known to have circulated in manuscript before around 1530. Of these, around twenty made it into print, selected according to availability and marketability, of which eight are among the older romances written before 1350. This reduction in numbers represents a narrowing of the tradition. But while not all the earlier romances came into print, it is certainly the case that printing extended the numbers of people who could afford their own copy. This, in itself, changed the nature of the reading

Figure 51. Translated and printed by William Caxton (probably with Colard Mansion) in Bruges in 1473 or 1474, *The Recuyell of the Historyes of Troye* is the first book printed in English. This copy's owner, George Horton, has inscribed his name above a passage in which Pantheus argues in vain against Paris's fateful mission to Greece to abduct Helen. Oxford, Bodleian Library, Arch. G d.1, fol. 263v.

experience, as well as opening up romance to a wider public. Yet it should be emphasized that there is not a simple symmetrical relationship here between high-status owners of earlier manuscripts and less affluent owners of printed books. Humbler readers and listeners, including servants, women and children, were among the users and audiences for fifteenth-century handwritten books of romance used and read within households. Likewise, readers from higher social levels were included among those who owned printed copies, such as Edward Duke of Buckingham (1478–1521), whose library contained several of de Worde's romances.

Figure 52. Wynkyn de Worde's 1509 print of *Richard Coeur de Lyon* is an inexpensive book by comparison with a deluxe manuscript; nevertheless the impression is that a good deal of care went into its preparation for the press, both through changes to the text and its visual layout. Here on the title page is a decorative woodcut illustration and ornamented border. Oxford, Bodleian Library, Crynes 734, fol. A.i r.

To have such a rich and eminent individual as Buckingham among his clients attests that de Worde was successful in his aim to maximize his readership. We can see that it made good business sense to cultivate readers from across the social spectrum and to cater, as far as possible, to both more wealthy and less affluent buyers. This entrepreneurial imperative is reflected in the material and textual forms of de Worde's printed books and can be observed, for example, in a copy of *Richard Coeur de Lyon* printed by de Worde in 1509 (Bodleian Library Crynes 734; figs 52 and 53). The small quarto size of the volume would have kept it within reach of a wide range of potential buyers, and it was certainly more affordable than the costly folio size books usually avoided by de Worde. Of course, cost and cheapness are relative, and even a quarto print would have been beyond the pockets of the poorest members of society. And while size brought down the cost, we can observe that this print of *Richard Coeur de Lyon* is by no means

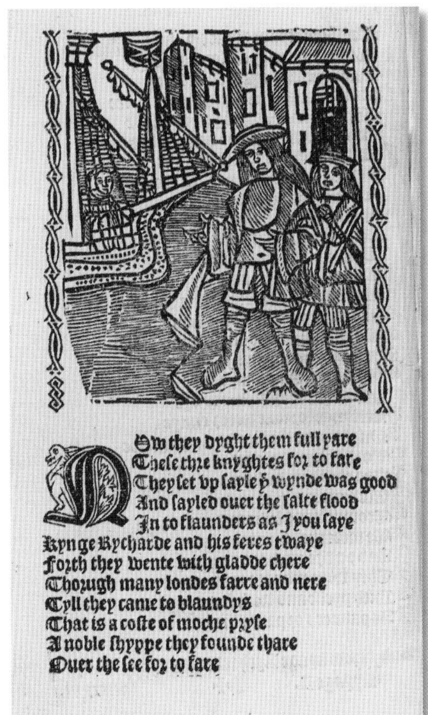

Now they dyght them full yare
Theſe thꝛe knyghtes foꝛ to fare
They ſet vp ſayle yͤ wynde was good
And ſayled ouer the ſalte flood
In to flaunders as I you ſaye
Kynge Rycharde and his feres twaye
Foꝛth they wente with gladde chere
Thoꝛugh many londes farre and nere
Tyll they came to blaundys
That is a coſte of moche pꝛyſe
A noble ſhyppe they founde thare
Ouer the ſee foꝛ to fare

Figure 53. This page from de Worde's *Richard Coeur de Lyon* includes a woodcut illustration with an ornamental border and decorative initial block. These techniques are of the kind routinely used by continental printers and, as can be seen here, give an attractive overall appearance to the page. Oxford, Bodleian Library, Crynes 734, fol. B.iii v.

the cheapest possible production. Carefully set out, it has many woodcuts to illustrate the story as well as attractive features of layout, such as paragraphing, decorative borders and block initials at narrative divisions. This attention to visual detail involved an investment of time and financial outlay that de Worde must have been confident was worthwhile. Further editorial endeavour is apparent in the many small-scale changes made to the language of the text: replacing archaic or difficult words, updating outmoded features of spelling and syntax, and thereby making the text more palatable for Tudor readers.[2] As well as these minute linguistic adjustments, there is a targeted series of excisions to remove story elements glorifying the Multon and D'Oyly families. These references, which appear in earlier versions of the romance, presumably seemed obscure to later audiences who were several decades out of touch with the once celebrated status of these families.[3] All of these editorial efforts anticipate buyers who expected a standard of quality and finish in the books they purchased. That there was a desire to cater to elite readers is further confirmed by the colophon in which de Worde emphasizes his association with Lady Margaret Beaufort: 'Thus endeth the story of the noble kynge Rycharde cuer de lyon. Enprynted at London in [th]e Fletestrete at the sygne of the sonne by Wynkyn de Worde / prynter vnto the moost excellent pryncesse my lady the kynges moder'.[4]

Unsurprisingly, given the rise of printing, far fewer handwritten copies of romance were produced after around 1500. Although this is not by any means to propose that the moment Caxton's first book came off the press in 1473, the era of handwriting was over. Existing handwritten copies of romance continued to be read and to reach new audiences, as is shown to us by the marginalia and inscriptions of sixteenth- and seventeenth-century readers.[5] At the same time, new handwritten books were produced in parallel with print, especially where there was no print version available of a particular romance. There is the case of Bodleian Library, MS Rawl. C. 86, a miscellaneous collection that includes two Arthurian romances not known to have made it into print: *Landeval* (a version of *Launfal*) and *The Wedding of Sir Gawain and Dame Ragnell* (fig. 54). The book is actually a collection of booklets, each copied around 1500 and subsequently bound together to form a codex. Their contents are typical of the tastes of middle-class, often mercantile, London readers and include works by Chaucer and practical and historical poems, alongside texts featuring metropolitan themes and locations, such as *Piers of Fulham*. Romance, particularly Arthurian romance, appealed to Tudor London readers, perhaps due to its affinities with national and civic pride, as well as its links with city pageants. These kinds of interests stimulated the regular and routine production of booklets in which romance was compiled along with a range of other texts that reflect these readers' outlooks and concerns.[6]

As well as relatively plain booklets such as those that make up MS Rawl. C. 86, Tudor manuscripts of romance included more costly bespoke commissions, such as Bodleian Library MS Ashmole 45. Hand-copied in London in the 1520s, MS Ashmole 45 originally contained just one text, *The Earl of Toulouse*, a Breton lay composed around 1400. The opening page is decorated with an attractive pen-and-ink illustration in which a man hands a book to a woman

Figure 54. The title 'The Weddynge of Sr Gawen & Dame Ragnell' has here been squeezed into available space as an afterthought. The scribe makes a mistake at the start of the text: he incorrectly copies a large 'R' and then has to start again with a large 'L' for the beginning of the first line 'Lythe and listenyth the lif of a lord riche' (Hark and listen to the life story of a rich lord!). Oxford, Bodleian Library, MS Rawl. C. 86, fol. 128v (England, late fifteenth century).

(fig. 55). It is unusual to have a presentation scene at the opening of a Middle English text. The man and the woman depicted are both wealthy bourgeoisie, as can be seen from the style of their rich clothing. The inscription within the scroll, 'Prenes: engre' (Take [this book] with pleasure), shows us that the volume was intended as a gift, perhaps from a husband to a wife, possibly a marriage gift.[7] It would certainly have made a fine present for a prosperous wife as it is both visually appealing and valuable: the copying by itself would have cost several shillings, far more than the few pence for one of de Worde's printed romances, and the illustration adds further quality and appeal. Moreover, *The Earl of Toulouse* seems ideally suited to a wife or bride, since its story, which deals with the innocence of a female protagonist, a persecuted and falsely accused Empress and wife, celebrates feminine strength and loyalty. It is a gift that carries meaning at the levels of its literary theme, visual form and the personal relations associated with the exchange.

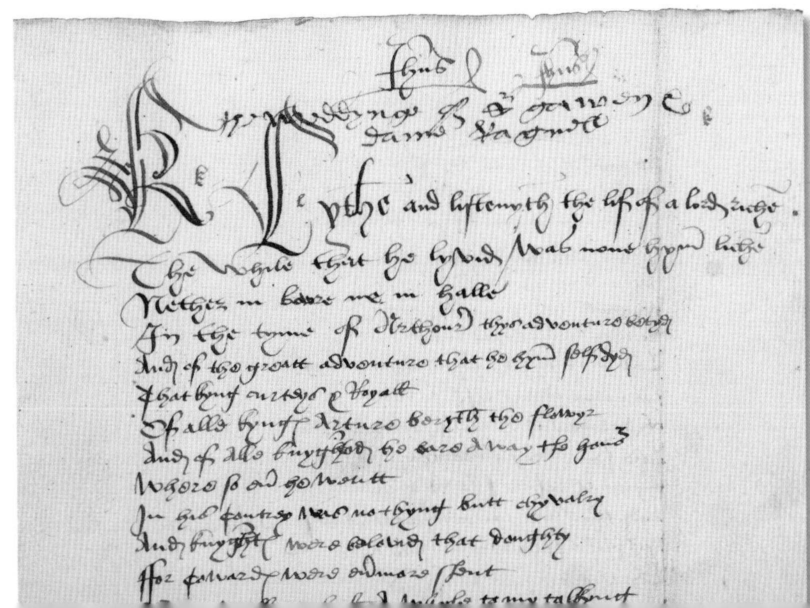

Wm Browne

The Story of the Isle of Calons

PRENES ENGRE

MD MARIA

Figure 55 *left*. In this beautiful presentation illustration, produced in London in the 1520s, a man hands a book to a woman with the words 'Take [this book] with pleasure'. Although the couple's identity is unknown, this copy of *The Earl of Toulouse* was seemingly intended as a gift for a wealthy female reader. Oxford, Bodleian Library, MS Ashmole 45, fol. 2r.

Figure 56. *The Earl of Toulouse* is set out in single columns skilfully decorated with enlarged calligraphic initials, as can be seen here at the start of the poem. The scribe has written his own name, Morgan ('morganus'), hidden in the folds of the scrolling decoration on the opening initial 'J' of this first line 'Jesu crist in trinite'. Oxford, Bodleian Library, MS Ashmole 45, fol. 3r.

These are not the only aspects of MS Ashmole 45 that provide clues to the circumstances of its production and reception. We know the name of the scribe was Morgan, as he writes this into the intertwining decoration of the opening initial, and that his initials were 'MD', as he interweaves these into the final paragraph symbol (figs 56 and 57). Morgan's highly professional style of handwriting shows us he was a legal scribe, most likely associated with the royal administration under Thomas Wolsey. His regular work would have allowed him to undertake occasional one-off commissions on demand, such as this one. It would also have brought him into contact with craftsmen of considerable calibre and accomplishment, which explains his remarkable collaboration with the skilled illustrator of the presentation scene, who was perhaps one of the favoured courtly Flemish artists of the day. A subsequent owner of the book, from the next generation, a man called William Fitzwilliam, used the blank pages following the romance to note down texts of interest and to write his life story (fig. 57). From these we can tell he was a man well connected within the mercantile and intellectual circles of sixteenth-century London society. All together, this combination of features – the affluent couple depicted in the illustration, the skilled professional scribe and artist, the well-connected later owner – help to place the volume securely within the upper echelons of Tudor metropolitan society.

While printing brought a wider public to medieval romance, MS Rawl. C. 86 and MS Ashmole 45 offer us a glimpse into the simultaneous and ongoing circulation of romance in manuscript form. However, as the sixteenth century progressed, handwritten books of romance become increasingly rare. Those that do survive tend to be idiosyncratic and, rather than a regular flow of production, they reflect the more specialized interests and eccentricities of their makers. There is the case of the book entirely hand-copied in 1564 by a man from Hampshire called Edward Bannister (1540–1606; Bodleian Library MS Douce 261).[8] It contains four medieval metrical romances, which Bannister copied out from their print versions: *Isumbras*, *Degaré*, *A Jeaste of Sir Gawayne* and *Eglamour of Artois*. Bannister painstakingly reproduced not only these texts in block letters, but also the illustrations that accompanied them. In this way he meticulously and systematically converted the prints back into manuscript form (figs 58 and 59). Bannister's motivation for this antiquarian project came not only from his literary interests, but was also an expression of his strong Catholic sympathies. That is to say, his enthusiasm for traditional romance in its manuscript form can be seen to reflect a nostalgia for an earlier era and for the old religion.[9]

Bannister's book indicates the appeal of medieval romance to recusants which is apparent elsewhere in the period, not least in

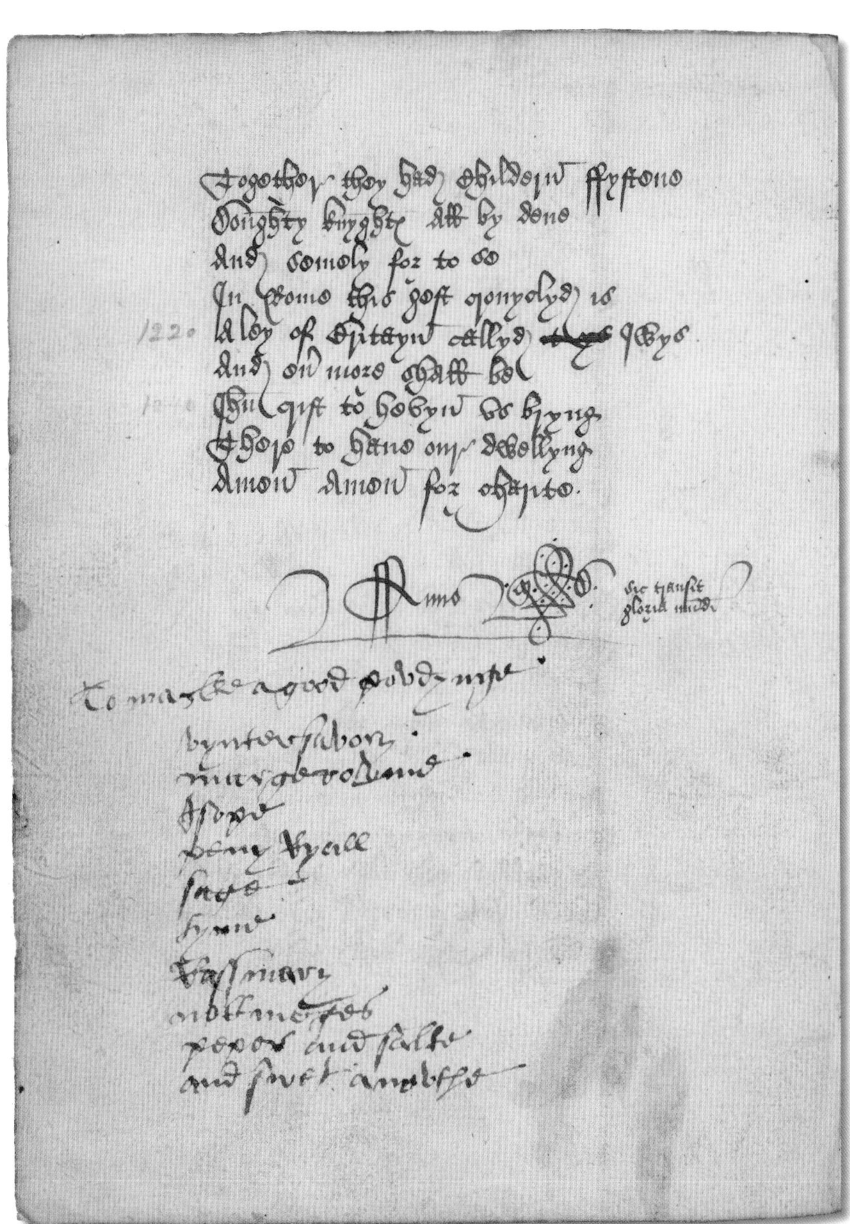

Figure 57. At the end of *The Earl of Toulouse* the scribe interweaves his initials 'M. D.' into the final paragraph symbol. Below the romance, William Fitzwilliam, a later sixteenth-century owner of the book, has added a recipe 'To macke a good povdynge'. Oxford, Bodleian Library, MS Ashmole 45, fol. 31v.

Here begynneth the hystorye of the
valyaunte Knyght Syr Isenbras

Figure 58. Amateur scribe Edward Bannister copied out not only the texts of printed romances, but also their illustrations. On the title page to *Isumbras*, the hero carries a staff of office on his shoulder. Whereas the text has hardly been updated, the image features contemporary clothing and a classical-style frame, the trumpeting figures at the top of which may stand for Isumbras's worldly wealth and pride. Oxford, Bodleian Library, MS Douce 261, fol. 1r.

its brief flourishing during Mary's reign (1553–58), when no fewer than twenty-two editions of medieval romances were printed by William Copland.[10] Many critics regarded medieval romances to be unsuitable reading material for pious Protestants – dangerously saturated with the Catholic ideology of the era in which they were written, evident from the many references to miracles, palmers, pilgrimages, holy sites, angels and hagiographical features, all of which permeate romance. While these criticisms were sustained, we should nevertheless keep this viewpoint in perspective. We must not forget that romance was criticized in its own era by commentators concerned about standards of pious reading, such as poet and cleric William of Nassyngton (d.1354), discussed in Chapter 3. Such attacks, while they are genuine and reflect contemporary concerns, must at the same time be recognized as rhetorical and conventional. Ultimately, the strength of Tudor and Elizabethan criticisms and condemnations themselves attest to how widely known medieval romance continued to be. Traditional

Figure 59. Bannister's careful attempt to replicate the details of his original can be seen in this illustration from *Eglamour of Artois*, which features a family in a domestic setting with two small dogs. Oxford, Bodleian Library, MS Douce 261, fols 27v–28r.

romance was everywhere, in pageants, plays, and visual and material culture, as well as continuing its long-standing associations with particular geographical locales – the most renowned being Bevis at Southampton, Guy at Warwick and Arthur at various sites. Monuments and objects, such as swords, tapestries, skulls and statues, were treasured at these locations because of spurious connections to these local and national romance heroes, whose

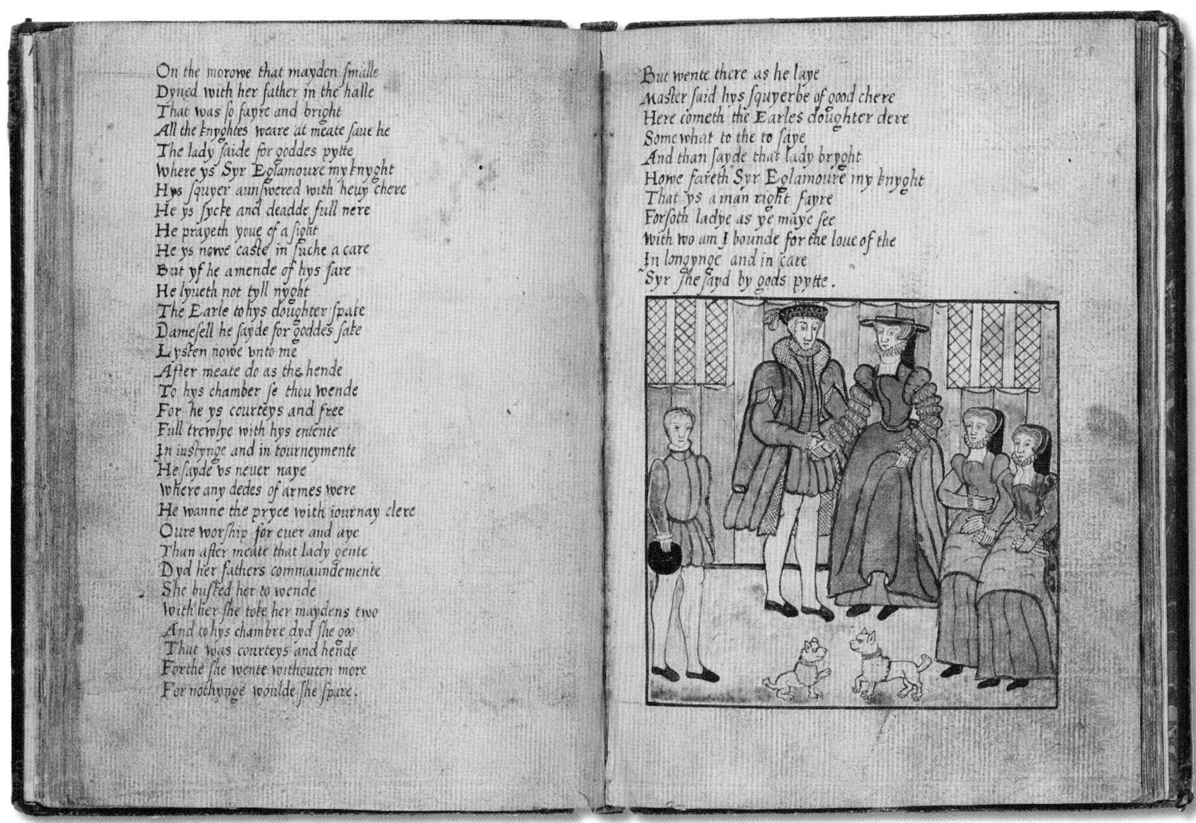

On the morowe that mayden ſmalle
Dyned with her father in the halle
That was ſo fayre and bright
All the knyghtes weare at meate ſaue he
The lady ſaide for goddes pytte
Where ys Syr Eglamoure my knyght
Hys ſquyer aunſwered with heuy chere
He ys ſycke and deadde full nere
He prayeth youe of a ſight
He ys nowe caſte in ſuche a care
But yf he amende of hys ſare
He lyueth not tyll nyght
The Earle to hys doughter ſpake
Dameſell he ſayde for goddes ſake
Lysten nowe vnto me
After meate do as the hende
To hys chamber ſe thou wende
For he ys courteys and free
Full trewlye with hys entente
In iustynge and in tourneymente
He ſayde vs neuer naye
Where any dedes of armes were
He wanne the pryce with iournay clere
Oure worſhip for euer and aye
Than after meate that lady gente
Dyd her fathers commaundemente
She buſked her to wende
With her ſhe toke her maydens two
And to hys chambre dyd ſhe goo
That was courteys and hende
Forthe ſhe wente withouten more
For nothynge woulde ſhe ſpare.

But wente there as he laye
Maſter ſaid hys ſquyer be of good chere
Here cometh the Earles doughter dere
Somewhat to the to ſaye
And than ſayde that lady bryght
Howe fareth Syr Eglamoure my knyght
That ys a man right fayre
Forſoth ladye as ye maye ſee
With wo am I bounde for the loue of the
In longynge and in care
Syr ſhe ſayd by gods pytte.

kyng arthur

exploits and achievements they functioned to record and validate. In these ways, romance was deeply and intensely woven into England's imagined history and geography (figs 60 and 61).

It is within this context of the ubiquity of traditional romance that we should imagine its reception. Many different kinds of readers owned collections of printed books of romance, the most famous example being that of Captain Cox, a Coventry mason and a performer of songs, ballads, traditional tales, poetry and chivalric romance. Cox's library is recorded in a letter by Robert Laneham, or Langham, on the occasion of Elizabeth I's visit to Kenilworth in 1575 and is generally regarded as 'the first important list of reading matter for the people'.[11] His library included eight copies of medieval verse romances alongside many other entertaining works, such as plays and jests, all of which he had 'at his fingers ends' ready to be recited and performed. Above all, Cox stands as a reminder of the vibrant oral tradition of romance that not only thrived but seemed to expand exponentially during the sixteenth century. Its traces are apparent to us today in various fleeting references and chance survivals, foremost among which is the Percy Folio (British Library, MS Additional 27879). Copied in the North West Midlands before 1650, its 520 pages and 195 verse items provide, as Helen Cooper has described, a rare record of the 'unofficial life' of romance well into the seventeenth century.[12]

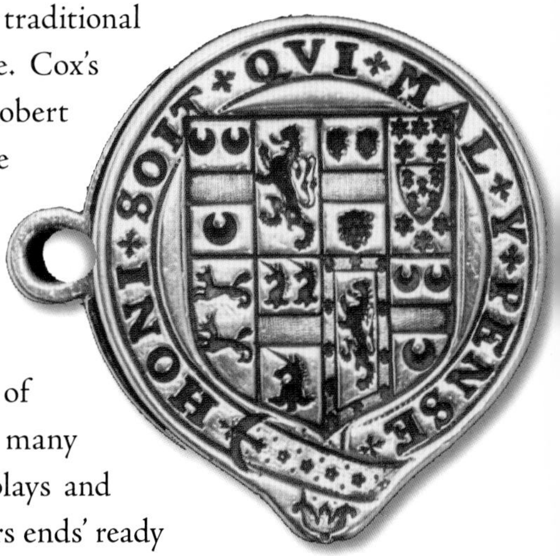

Figure 60 *left*. he magnificent round table that hangs in Winchester Great Hall was probably made for an Arthurian tournament during Edward I's reign (1272–1307). It was repaired and repainted at another highpoint of Arthurian interest under Henry VIII (probably in 1516), hence the prominent Tudor rose and King Arthur's passing resemblance to Henry. The Great Hall, Winchester © Hampshire County Council.

Figure 61. This small personal seal belonged to Sir Henry Lee (1533–1611), and was probably made when he became a Knight of the Garter in 1597. It shows his coat of arms bordered by a garter ribbon, inscribed with its motto 'Honi soit qui mal y pense'. Henry Lee was prominent in the court's festive events such as the annual Accession Day tilts – chivalric revival tournaments that celebrated Elizabeth I's accession. Photo © Victoria and Albert Museum, London.

Among its various items are eight versions of medieval romances, including *Eglamour of Artois, Degaré, Lambewell* (a version of *Launfal*) and *Lybeaus Desconus.* In addition to these are a number of more drastically, some would say disastrously, adapted versions of romance, such as *The Grene Knight.* In this reworking of *Sir Gawain and the Green Knight* the story is stripped down to its bare essentials and retold in a popularized mode and verse form. Far from the elite setting of the medieval masterpiece *Sir Gawain and the Green Knight,* with its intricate virtuoso contemplations on spirituality, life, poetry and art, *The Grene Knight* presents the same story opened up to a popular mode and milieu.

This kind of recasting of romance for recitation and song is found elsewhere in the period in the numerous ballads printed to be sung to well-known tunes and pinned up on the walls of shops, cottages and ale-houses. These oral and popularized renditions of romance were among those targeted for mockery and disapproval by the humanist educated elite. Literary satirists and cultural critics ridiculed romance for its failure to match up to current fashionable standards of rhetorical eloquence. George Puttenham in 1589 lists Guy of Warwick as one of the 'old romances' that could be heard sung 'by blind harpers or such like taverne minstrels' who will 'give a fit of mirth for a groat' (give you an entertaining song for a groat [worth four pence]).[13] No doubt Puttenham would have sneered at the Percy Folio's spin-off renditions of famous episodes from the life of Guy of Warwick: *Guy and Colbrande,* which features Guy's defeat of the giant Colbrond, and *Guy and Philis,* which recounts the love-story element of the romance. He would doubtless have turned up his nose at the broadside ballad version of *Guy of Warwick* registered to Richard Jones in 1592 to be sung to the tune of 'was ever man soe tost in love'.[14] Even more scathing and contemptuous is Thomas Nashe's criticism of jejune romance and its 'worn-out absurdities'. Nashe goes so far as to provide a list, for the amusement of his readers, of examples of poor style from the print version of *Bevis of Hamtoun*:

> *The porter said, by my snout,*
> *It was Sir Bevis that I let out.*
>
> or this,
> *He smote his son on the breast,*
> *That he never after spoke with clerk or priest.*
>
> or this,
> *This alms, by my crown,*
> *Gives she for Bevis of South-hamptown.*
>
> or this,
> *Some lost a nose, some a lip,*
> *And the King of Scots hath a ship.*

'Who is it', Nashe asks, citing these sloppy and desperate attempts to hold together the verse form, 'that reading *Bevis of Hamtoun*, can forbeare laughing, if he mark what scambling shift he makes to end his verses alike?'[15] Criticized on the one hand on moral and religious grounds, on the other it became *de rigueur* to deride medieval romance for its apparent literary failings and perceived naiveties.

Despite these snipes and criticisms, it is important to emphasize that the story of romance in the age of print is not a simple narrative of decline and descent, nor a falling arc into cultural oblivion.

In reality, there was a much more irregular pattern according to which some versions of romance were inclusive and known to all members of society, whereas others were restricted to elite circles. That is to say, while printing and the oral tradition ensured native romance was disseminated across all social sectors, it nevertheless retained a level of cultural capital that gave it buoyancy within the Elizabethan social and literary elite. This is vividly apparent in the writings of aspiring courtier Edmund Spenser (1552–99), who was deeply influenced by and knowledgeable about native romance. His career-defining epic poem *The Faerie Queene* (1590, 1596) is both a romance and a dialogue with romance. Right from its opening line, 'A Gentle Knight was pricking on the plaine', it invokes a rich fabric of romance structures, motifs, conventions and antiquated linguistic forms, which are imaginatively combined in a bewildering web of intertextual references. Book I owes specific verbal debt to the dragon-slaying episode from *Bevis of Hamtoun* and exploits the romance types of 'slandered ladies' and 'displaced youths'. The figure of the Redcrosse Knight provides an ironic take on the convention of 'the fair unknown', whereby the notion of nobility by birth, and of being specially chosen from birth to be destined for greatness, is explored in relation to the Calvinist doctrine of the Elect. In this way Spenser exploits the versatility and enduring appeal of the fair unknown – which continues to this day, more recently re-embodied as Luke Skywalker and Harry Potter. Book II is likewise deeply embedded in native romance, this time the story of *Guy of Warwick*. Guy transmutes into Spenser's Sir Guyon, and his well-worn tale allows for investigation of the true meanings of chivalry and pilgrimage as expressions of Christian knighthood.[16]

Figure 62. Sir Thomas Posthumous Hoby claims his ownership of this copy of *The Faerie Queene* (printed by William Ponsonbie, 1590) by adding his signature here on the title page: 'T:Posth:Hoby:'. Oxford, Bodleian Library, F 2.62 Linc, title page.

Through such engagements with native romance, Spenser acknowledges a series of displacements between the religious and moral concerns of his own day and those of the nation's native history and literature. Crucially, the agenda of *The Faerie Queene* expects readers to recognize England's native romance tradition in order to transform romance for the nation. Spenser relies on both his readers' familiarity with the wider literary tradition and their memory of the detail of specific romances which underpin particular sections and aspects of the poem. We can gain a glimpse

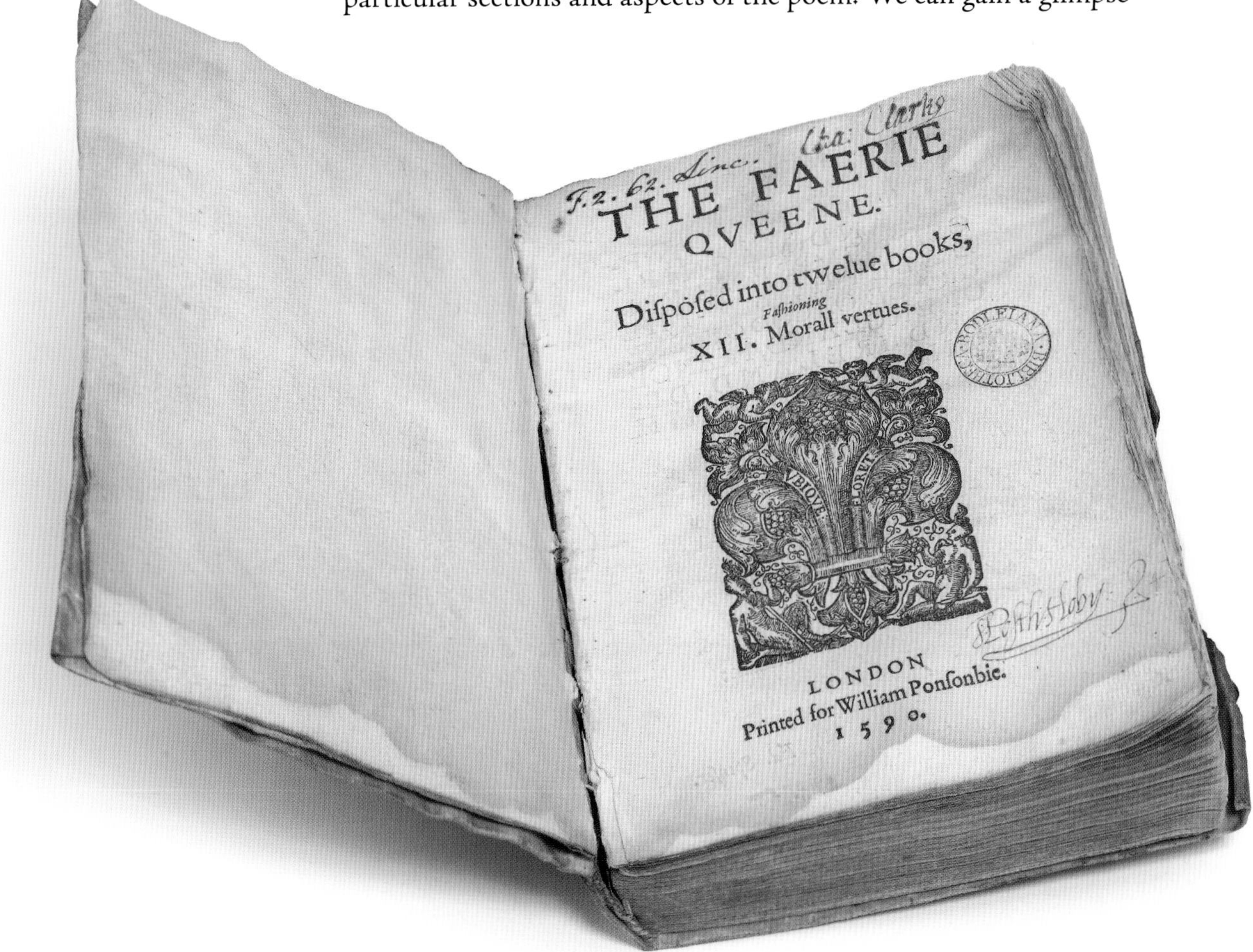
THE FAERIE
QVEENE.
Diſpoſed into twelue books,
Faſhioning
XII. Morall vertues.

LONDON
Printed for William Ponſonbie.
1590.

of this readership in a copy of *The Faerie Queene* printed in 1590 and now held at the Bodleian Library. It was owned by Sir Thomas Posthumous Hoby (1566–1644), who signs his name on the title page and adds annotations to Books I and II summarizing the story (figs 62 and 63). He was the second son of Sir Thomas Hoby, courtier and translator of Castiglione's *The Book of the Courtier* (1561), and Elizabeth Cooke Hoby (later Lady Russell), a highly learned woman who published a translation of a treatise on the sacrament in 1605. A further literary connection comes from Hoby's wife, Lady Margaret Dakins Hoby (1571–1633), the first Englishwoman known to have written a diary. Hoby himself is known for his involvement in local politics, as JP and MP for Hackness in North Yorkshire, and for his reputation as a fierce and humourless Puritan opponent to the

Figure 63. Posthumous Hoby adds numerous annotations to *The Faerie Queene*. Here in Book II, Canto III his marginal notes summarize the story and help him to keep track of Spenser's complicated, often disorientating narrative. Oxford, Bodleian Library, F 2.62 Linc, pp. 218–19.

local Catholic gentry.[17] Like Spenser, Hoby had received all the benefits of a humanist education at the same time as having grown up as part of a generation who were immersed in native romance through its continual and pervasive presence in the culture. It is difficult to imagine that, as a reader of *The Faerie Queene*, he could have failed to be alert to its invocations of this literary tradition, or its resonance with contemporary political and religious concerns, with which he was fully involved.

Shakespeare, like Spenser, engages extensively with romance and expects his audiences to recognize the romance structures and motifs that appear scattered throughout his plays. In some cases we are able to track the origins of a particular play through to its medieval past. There is the medieval romance *Gamelyn*, adapted in 1588 by Thomas Lodge as *Rosalynde, Euphues Golden Legacy*, the major source for Shakespeare's romantic pastoral comedy *As You Like It* (1599; figs 64 and 65). Another example is the Greek story of Apollonius of Tyre, known from Old and Middle English romance; from John Gower's *Confessio amantis* (*c.*1390 and prints); from the Latin *Gesta Romanorum* (continually printed from *c.*1475); from de Worde's *Kynge Apollyn of Thyre* (1510); from Lawrence Twine's *The Pattern of Painfull Adventures* (1576); and then, eventually, from George Wilkins's *The Painfull Adventures of Pericles* (1608), which is closely linked to *Pericles*, thought to be co-written by Shakespeare and Wilkins (fig. 66). Modern critics and audiences have tended to struggle with the staging and interpretation of *Pericles*. However, its convoluted story of shipwrecks, pirates, separated families and sexual conundrums would have been instantly recognizable to early audiences. *Pericles* is, in fact, one of four plays written late

Euphues

(quoth Ginimede) what mad cattel you women be, whose harts sometimes are made of Adamant that wil touch with no impression, and sometime of wax that is fit for euery forme: they delight to be courted, and then they glory to seeme coy, and when they are most desired then they freese with disdaine: and this fault is so common to the sex, that you see it painted out in the shepheardes passions, who found his Mistres as froward as he was enamoured. And I pray you (quoth Aliena) if your robes were off, what mettal are you made of that you are so satyrical against women? Is it not a foule bird defiles the own nest? Beware (Ganimede) that Rosader heare you not, if hee doo, perchance you wil make him leape so farre from loue, that he wil anger euery vaine in your heart. Thus (quoth Ganimede) I keepe decorum, I speak now as I am Alienas Page, not as I am Gerismonds daughter: for put mee but into a peticoat, and I wil stand in defiance to the vttermost, that women are curteous, constant, vertuous, and what not. Stay there (quoth Aliena) and no more words, for yonder be Caracters grauen vppon the barke of the tall Beech tree: let vs see (quoth Ganimede): and with that they read a fancy written to this effect.

First shall the heauens want starry light,
The seas be robbed of their waues:
The day want sunne, and sunne want bright,
The night want shade, the dead mens graues.
The April, flowers and leafe and tree,
Before I false my faith to thee.

First shall the tops of highest hils
By humble plaines be ouerpride:
And Poets scorne the Muses quils,
And fish forsake the water glide.
And Iris *loose her coloured weed,*
Before I faile thee at thy need.

First direful hate shall turne to peace,
And loue relent in deepe disdaine:

And

golden Legacie.

And Poets scorne the Muses quils,
And fish forsake the water glide,
And Iris *loose her coloured weed,*
Before I faile thee at thy need.

First direfull hate shall turn to peace,
And loue relent in deep disdain:
And death his fatall stroake shall cease,
And enuy pitie euery paine.
And pleasure mourn, and sorow smile,
Before I talke of any guile.

First time shall stay his staylesse race,
And winter blesse his browes with corne:
And snow bemoysten Julies face,
And winter spring, and sommer mourn,
Before my pen by helpe of fame,
Cease to recite thy sacred name.
Montanus.

No doubt (quoth Ganimede) this protestation grew from one full of passions. I am of that minde too (quoth Aliena) but see I pray, when poore women seeke to keepe themselues chaste, how men woo them with many fained promises, alluring with sweet words as the Syrens, and after proouing as trothlesse as Aeneas. Thus promised Demophoon to his Phillis, but who at last grew more false? The reason was (quoth Ganimede) that they were womens sonnes, and tooke that fault of their mother, for if man had growne from man, as Adam did from the earth, men had neuer been troubled with inconstancie. Leaue off (quoth Aliena) to taunt thus bitterly, or els ile pull off your pages apparell and whip you (as Venus doth her wantons) with nettles. So you will (quoth Ganimede) perswade mee to flattery, and that needs not: but come (seeing we haue found here by this Fount the tract of Shepheardes by their Madrigalles and Roundelaies) let vs forwarde: for either wee shall finde some foldes, sheepcoates, or els some cottages wherein for a day or two

E to

Figure 64 *left.* Thomas Lodge's romance *Rosalynde* (printed in London by Abel Ieffes for T. Gubbin and Iohn Busbie, 1592), is best known today as the source of Shakespeare's *As You Like It*, but its own success is apparent from its numerous reprintings. Written whilst Lodge was on a piratical expedition to the Canary Isles, it markets itself as a newly found text and includes Euphues's alleged instructions to the finder: 'If any man find this scrowle, send it to Philautus in England'. Oxford, Bodleian Library, Mal. 152(1), fol. D4v–E1r.

Figure 65. *As You Like It*, from the 1623 first folio edition of Shakespeare's *Comedies, Histories, and Tragedies*. The play mingles a romance plot of family disputes and exile with adventures in young love, gender reversals and pastoral comedy. Oxford, Bodleian Library, Arch. G c. 8, pp. 194–5.

in Shakespeare's career often referred to as his 'romances' because of their indebtedness to traditional themes and motifs: *Pericles* (1607–08), *Cymbeline* (1609–10), *The Winter's Tale* (1610–11) and *The Tempest* (1611).[18] Their composition coincides with a move to a different theatre and a more courtly audience, to which they seem to have been designed to appeal. And whereas earlier critics tended to dismiss them as fairy tales, more recent and serious attention acknowledges their powerful engagements with issues of colonial expansion, the purpose of travel, rulership, feminist ethics, melancholy and sexual morality. For Shakespeare, his audience and his

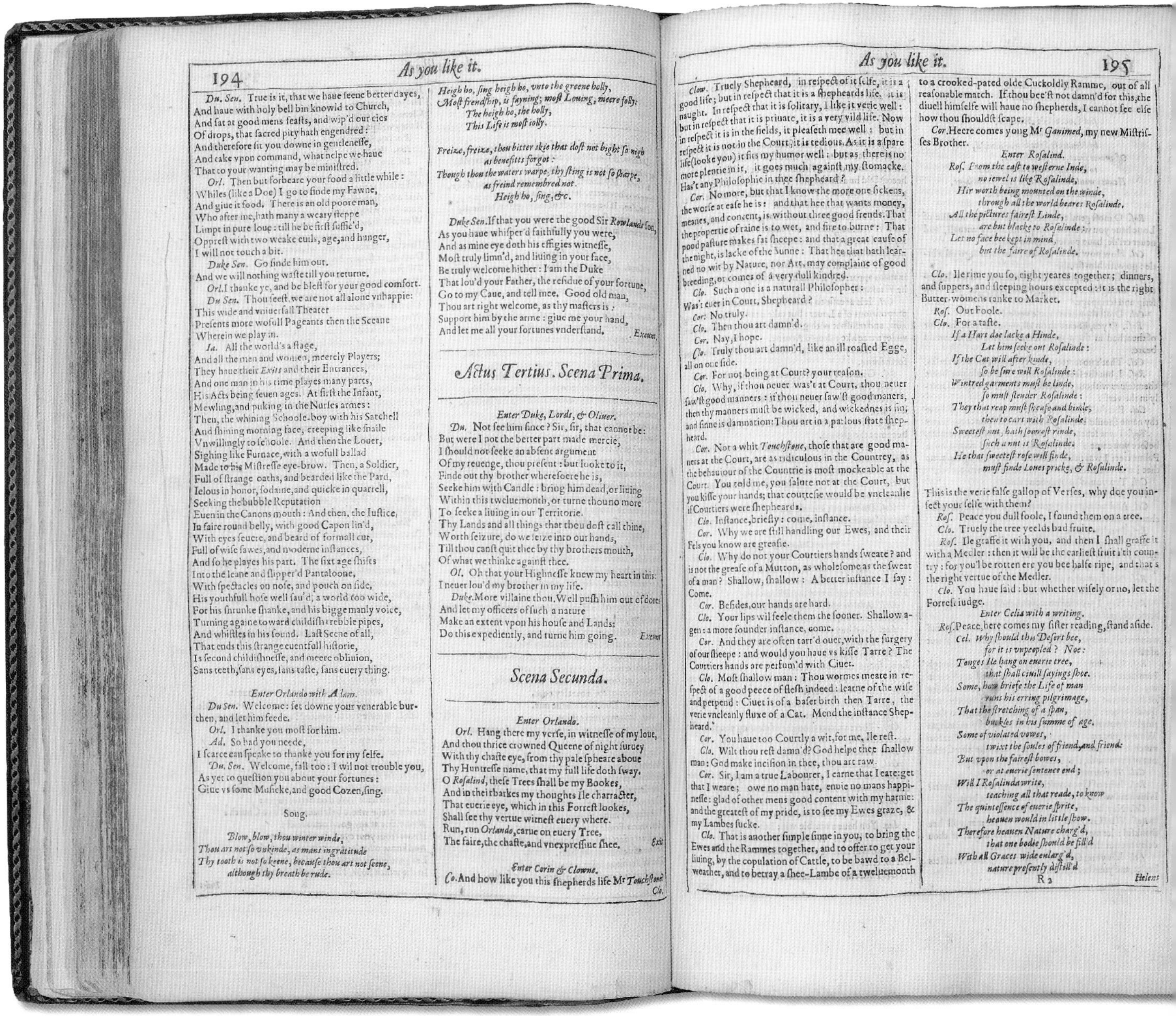

194 *As you like it.*

Du. Sen. True is it, that we haue seene better dayes,
And haue with holy bell bin knowld to Church,
And sat at good mens feasts, and wip'd our eies
Of drops, that sacred pity hath engendred:
And therefore sit you downe in gentlenesse,
And take vpon command, what helpe we haue
That to your wanting may be ministred.

Orl. Then but forbeare your food a little while:
Whiles (like a Doe) I go to finde my Fawne,
And giue it food. There is an old poore man,
Who after me, hath many a weary steppe
Limpt in pure loue: till he be first suffic'd,
Opprest with two weake euils, age, and hunger,
I will not touch a bit.

Duke Sen. Go finde him out.
And we will nothing waste till you returne.

Orl. I thanke ye, and be blest for your good comfort.

Du Sen. Thou seest, we are not all alone vnhappie:
This wide and vniuersall Theater
Presents more wofull Pageants then the Sceane
Wherein we play in.

Ia. All the world's a stage,
And all the men and women, meerely Players;
They haue their *Exits* and their Entrances,
And one man in his time playes many parts,
His Acts being seuen ages. At first the Infant,
Mewling, and puking in the Nurses armes:
Then, the whining Schoole-boy with his Satchell
And shining morning face, creeping like snaile
Vnwillingly to schoole. And then the Louer,
Sighing like Furnace, with a wofull ballad
Made to his Mistresse eye-brow. Then, a Soldier,
Full of strange oaths, and bearded like the Pard,
Ielous in honor, sodaine, and quicke in quarrell,
Seeking the bubble Reputation
Euen in the Canons mouth: And then, the Iustice,
In faire round belly, with good Capon lin'd,
With eyes seuere, and beard of formall cut,
Full of wise sawes, and moderne instances,
And so he playes his part. The sixt age shifts
Into the leane and slipper'd Pantaloone,
With spectacles on nose, and pouch on side,
His youthfull hose well sau'd, a world too wide,
For his shrunke shanke, and his bigge manly voice,
Turning againe toward childish trebble pipes,
And whistles in his sound. Last Scene of all,
That ends this strange euentfull historie,
Is second childishnesse, and meere obliuion,
Sans teeth, sans eyes, sans taste, sans euery thing.

Enter Orlando with Adam.

Du Sen. Welcome: set downe your venerable burthen, and let him feede.

Orl. I thanke you most for him.

Ad. So had you neede,
I scarce can speake to thanke you for my selfe.

Du. Sen. Welcome, fall too: I wil not trouble you,
As yet to question you about your fortunes:
Giue vs some Musicke, and good Cozen, sing.

Song.

Blow, blow, thou winter winde,
Thou art not so vnkinde, as mans ingratitude
Thy tooth is not so keene, because thou art not seene,
although thy breath be rude.
Heigh ho, sing heigh ho, vnto the greene holly,
Most frendship, is fayning; most Louing, meere folly:
The heigh ho, the holly,
This Life is most iolly.

Freize, freize, thou bitter skie that dost not bight so nigh
as benefitts forgot:
Though thou the waters warpe, thy sting is not so sharpe,
as freind remembred not.
Heigh ho, sing, &c.

Duke Sen. If that you were the good Sir *Rowlands* son,
As you haue whisper'd faithfully you were,
And as mine eye doth his effigies witnesse,
Most truly limn'd, and liuing in your face,
Be truly welcome hither: I am the Duke
That lou'd your Father, the residue of your fortune,
Go to my Caue, and tell mee. Good old man,
Thou art right welcome, as thy masters is:
Support him by the arme: giue me your hand,
And let me all your fortunes vnderstand. *Exeunt.*

Actus Tertius. Scena Prima.

Enter Duke, Lords, & Oliuer.

Du. Not see him since? Sir, sir, that cannot be:
But were I not the better part made mercie,
I should not seeke an absent argument
Of my reuenge, thou present: but looke to it,
Finde out thy brother wheresoere he is,
Seeke him with Candle: bring him dead, or liuing
Within this tweluemonth, or turne thou no more
To seeke a liuing in our Territorie.
Thy Lands and all things that thou dost call thine,
Worth seizure, do we seize into our hands,
Till thou canst quit thee by thy brothers mouth,
Of what we thinke against thee.

Ol. Oh that your Highnesse knew my heart in this:
I neuer lou'd my brother in my life.

Duke. More villaine thou. Well push him out of dores
And let my officers of such a nature
Make an extent vpon his house and Lands:
Do this expediently, and turne him going. *Exeunt*

Scena Secunda.

Enter Orlando.

Orl. Hang there my verse, in witnesse of my loue,
And thou thrice crowned Queene of night suruey
With thy chaste eye, from thy pale spheare aboue
Thy Huntresse name, that my full life doth sway.
O *Rosalind*, these Trees shall be my Bookes,
And in their barkes my thoughts Ile charracter,
That euerie eye, which in this Forrest lookes,
Shall see thy vertue witnest euery where.
Run, run *Orlando*, carue on euery Tree,
The faire, the chaste, and vnexpressiue shee. *Exit*

Enter Corin & Clowne.

Co. And how like you this shepherds life Mr *Touchstone*?

Clo.

As you like it. 195

Clow. Truely Shepheard, in respect of it selfe, it is a good life; but in respect that it is a shepheards life, it is naught. In respect that it is solitary, I like it verie well: but in respect that it is priuate, it is a very vild life. Now in respect it is in the fields, it pleaseth mee well: but in respect it is not in the Court, it is tedious. As it is a spare life (looke you) it fits my humor well: but as there is no more plentie in it, it goes much against my stomacke. Has't any Philosophie in thee shepheard?

Cor. No more, but that I know the more one sickens, the worse at ease he is: and that hee that wants money, meanes, and content, is without three good frends. That the propertie of raine is to wet, and fire to burne: That pood pasture makes fat sheepe: and that a great cause of the night, is lacke of the Sunne: That hee that hath learned no wit by Nature, nor Art, may complaine of good breeding, or comes of a very dull kindred.

Clo. Such a one is a naturall Philosopher:
Was't euer in Court, Shepheard?

Cor: No truly.

Clo. Then thou art damn'd.

Cor. Nay, I hope.

Clo. Truly thou art damn'd, like an ill roasted Egge, all on one side.

Cor. For not being at Court? your reason.

Clo. Why, if thou neuer was't at Court, thou neuer saw'st good manners: if thou neuer saw'st good maners, then thy manners must be wicked, and wickednes is sin, and sinne is damnation: Thou art in a parlous state shepheard.

Cor. Not a whit *Touchstone*, those that are good maners at the Court, are as ridiculous in the Countrey, as the behauiour of the Countrie is most mockeable at the Court. You told me, you salute not at the Court, but you kisse your hands; that courtesie would be vncleanlie if Courtiers were shepheards.

Clo. Instance, briefly: come, instance.

Cor. Why we are still handling our Ewes, and their Fels you know are greasie.

Clo. Why do not your Courtiers hands sweate? and is not the grease of a Mutton, as wholesome as the sweat of a man? Shallow, shallow: A better instance I say: Come.

Cor. Besides, our hands are hard.

Clo. Your lips wil feele them the sooner. Shallow agen: a more sounder instance, come.

Cor. And they are often tarr'd ouer, with the surgery of our sheepe: and would you haue vs kisse Tarre? The Courtiers hands are perfum'd with Ciuet.

Clo. Most shallow man: Thou wormes meate in respect of a good peece of flesh indeed: learne of the wise and perpend: Ciuet is of a baser birth then Tarre, the verie vncleanly fluxe of a Cat. Mend the instance Shepheard.

Cor. You haue too Courtly a wit, for me, Ile rest.

Clo. Wilt thou rest damn'd? God helpe thee shallow man: God make incision in thee, thou art raw.

Cor. Sir, I am a true Labourer, I earne that I eate: get that I weare; owe no man hate, enuie no mans happinesse: glad of other mens good content with my harme: and the greatest of my pride, is to see my Ewes graze, & my Lambes sucke.

Clo. That is another simple sinne in you, to bring the Ewes and the Rammes together, and to offer to get your liuing, by the copulation of Cattle, to be bawd to a Belweather, and to betray a shee-Lambe of a tweluemonth to a crooked-pated olde Cuckoldly Ramme, out of all reasonable match. If thou bee'st not damn'd for this, the diuell himselfe will haue no shepherds, I cannot see else how thou shouldst scape.

Cor. Heere comes yong Mr *Ganimed*, my new Mistrisses Brother.

Enter Rosalind.

Ros. From the east to westerne Inde,
no iewel is like Rosalinde,
Hir worth being mounted on the winde,
through all the world beares Rosalinde.
All the pictures fairest Linde,
are but blacke to Rosalinde:
Let no face bee kept in mind,
but the faire of Rosalinde.

Clo. Ile rime you so, eight yeares together; dinners, and suppers, and sleeping hours excepted: it is the right Butter-womens ranke to Market.

Ros. Out Foole.

Clo. For a taste.
If a Hart doe lacke a Hinde,
Let him seeke out Rosalinde:
If the Cat will after kinde,
so be sure will Rosalinde:
Wintred garments must be linde,
so must slender Rosalinde:
They that reap must sheafe and binde,
then to cart with Rosalinde.
Sweetest nut, hath sowrest rinde,
such a nut is Rosalinde.
He that sweetest rose will finde,
must finde Loues pricke, & Rosalinde.

This is the verie false gallop of Verses, why doe you infect your selfe with them?

Ros. Peace you dull foole, I found them on a tree.

Clo. Truely the tree yeelds bad fruite.

Ros. Ile graffe it with you, and then I shall graffe it with a Medler: then it will be the earliest fruit i'th country: for you'l be rotten ere you bee halfe ripe, and that's the right vertue of the Medler.

Clo. You haue said: but whether wisely or no, let the Forrest iudge.

Enter Celia with a writing.

Ros. Peace, here comes my sister reading, stand aside.

Cel. Why should this Desert bee,
for it is vnpeopled? Noe:
Tonges Ile hang on euerie tree,
that shall ciuill sayings shoe.
Some, how briefe the Life of man
runs his erring pilgrimage,
That the stretching of a span,
buckles in his summe of age.
Some of violated vowes,
twixt the soules of friend, and friend:
But vpon the fairest bowes,
or at euerie sentence end;
Will I Rosalinda write,
teaching all that reade, to know
The quintessence of euerie sprite,
heauen would in little show.
Therefore heauen Nature charg'd,
that one bodie should be fill'd
With all Graces wide enlarg'd,
nature presently distill'd

R 2 *Helens*

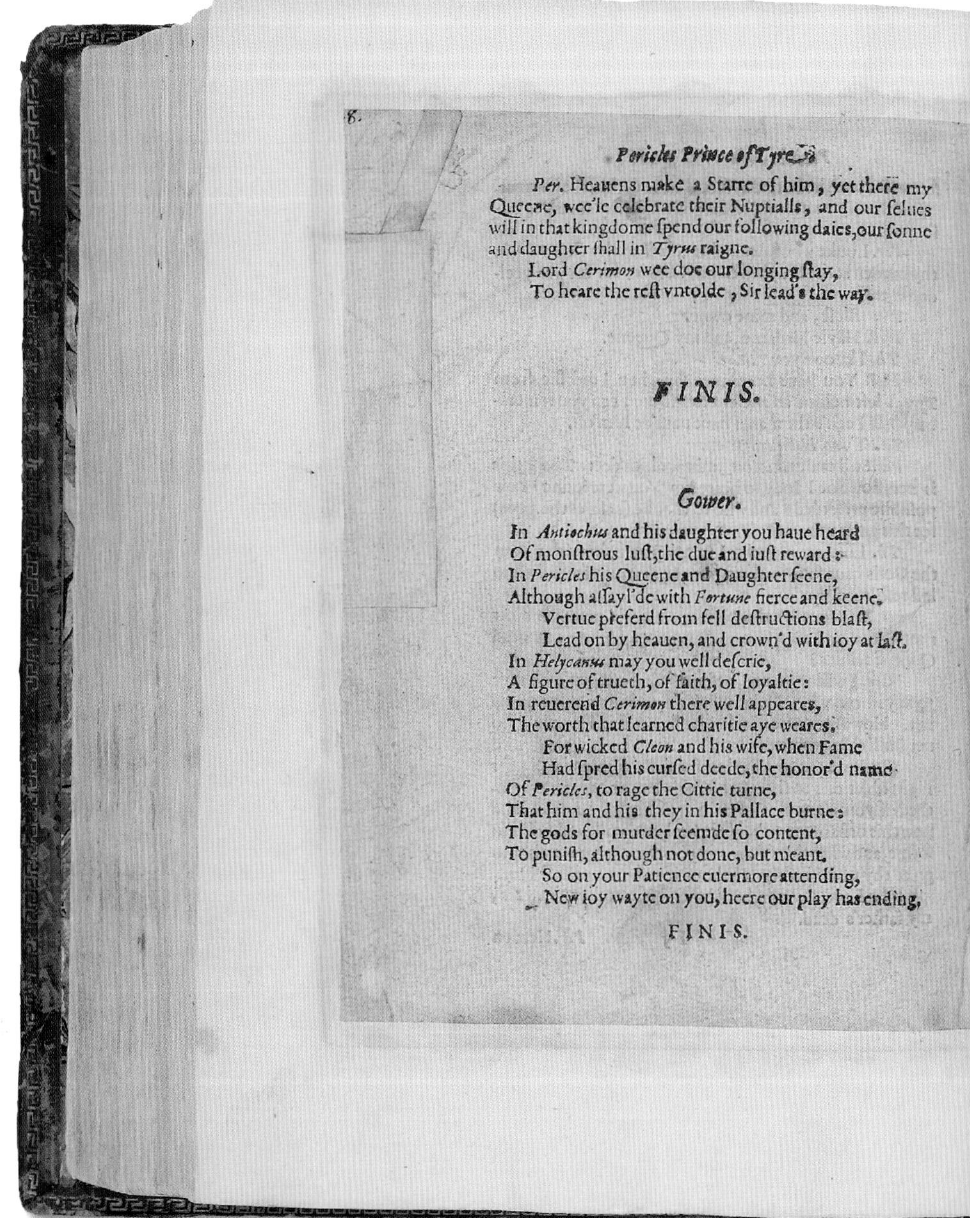

Pericles Prince of Tyre.

Per. Heauens make a Starre of him, yet there my Queene, wee'le celebrate their Nuptialls, and our ſelues will in that kingdome ſpend our following daies, our ſonne and daughter ſhall in *Tyrus* raigne.

Lord *Cerimon* wee doe our longing ſtay,
To heare the reſt vntolde, Sir lead's the way.

FINIS.

Gower.

In *Antiochus* and his daughter you haue heard
Of monſtrous luſt, the due and iuſt reward:
In *Pericles* his Queene and Daughter ſeene,
Although aſſayl'de with *Fortune* fierce and keene,
Vertue preferd from fell deſtructions blaſt,
Lead on by heauen, and crown'd with ioy at laſt.
In *Helycanus* may you well deſcrie,
A figure of trueth, of faith, of loyaltie:
In reuerend *Cerimon* there well appeares,
The worth that learned charitie aye weares.
For wicked *Cleon* and his wife, when Fame
Had ſpred his curſed deede, the honor'd name
Of *Pericles*, to rage the Cittie turne,
That him and his they in his Pallace burne:
The gods for murder ſeemde ſo content,
To puniſh, although not done, but meant.
So on your Patience euermore attending,
New ioy wayte on you, heere our play has ending.

FINIS.

Figure 66. *Pericles*, written partly by Shakespeare, was first published in an unauthorized quarto edition by Henry Gosson in 1609. Here we see the end of this edition and the title page of the 1619 quarto, bound into a volume of Shakespeariana by a later owner. Oxford, Bodleian Library, Arch. G d.41 (5), and Arch. G d.41 (6).

THE LATE, And much admired Play, CALLED, Pericles, Prince of Tyre.

With the true Relation of the whole History, aduentures, and fortunes of the saide Prince.

Written by W. SHAKESPEARE.

Printed for *T. P.* 1619.

generation, the traditional themes and motifs of romance provided a rich source of materials that could be shaped for the great literature and debates of the age.

The works of Shakespeare and Spenser are built upon a literary and linguistic foundation which is distinctively characterized by native English romance, yet which is presented through the classical and humanist mode. There are many other such literary engagements with native romance, especially those in which the famous figures from English history such as Guy, Bevis and Arthur continued to have key roles. There is the drama *The Tragical History of Guy of Warwick* (*c.*1590), where the romance is refashioned to resemble a Renaissance play through numerous expansions, which include a clown called Sparrow from Stratford-upon-Avon and an appearance from Oberon and his fairies. And there is Samuel Rowlands' *The Famous Historie of Guy of Warwick* (1609), which retells Guy's story in a Spenserian-inspired format and with a veneer of classical allusions designed to flatter the pretensions of his audience.[19] In these and other ways, and with greater or lesser degrees of success, romance was remoulded for Renaissance readers and audiences. The imperative to overlay and interweave classical references and humanistic touches with a distinctively English tradition of romance is encapsulated by an Elizabethan notebook held at the Bodleian Library (MS Greaves 60; fig. 67). Here we find transcribed sections from the alliterative Middle English romance *Alexander* interspersed with Latin exercises (the Latin on this page is a transcription of Gaius Sulpicius Apollinaris's synopsis that appears at the head of Roman dramatist Terence's comedy *Andria*). It provides for us a literal and visual illustration of the way native medieval romance

Figure 67. This Elizabethan notebook from around 1600 was part of the collection of Thomas Greaves (1612–76), an orientalist and reader of Arabic who studied at Corpus Christi College, Oxford. Sections from the medieval alliterative verse romance *Alexander* are interspersed with Latin exercises. Oxford, Bodleian Library, MS Greaves 60, fols 6v–7r.

was interwoven with the classics in Renaissance England, as a result of which the culture and literature were revitalized. We do not know the identity of this writer, but he or she stands for the last generation who grew up with both native romance and a humanist education. In the era between Caxton and Shakespeare medieval romance was transformed at the levels of language, materiality and literary themes and structures. In its new shapes and forms, and in its individual material and literary manifestations, we are reminded that the story of romance is intimately connected to the larger stories of printing, religious reform and humanism.

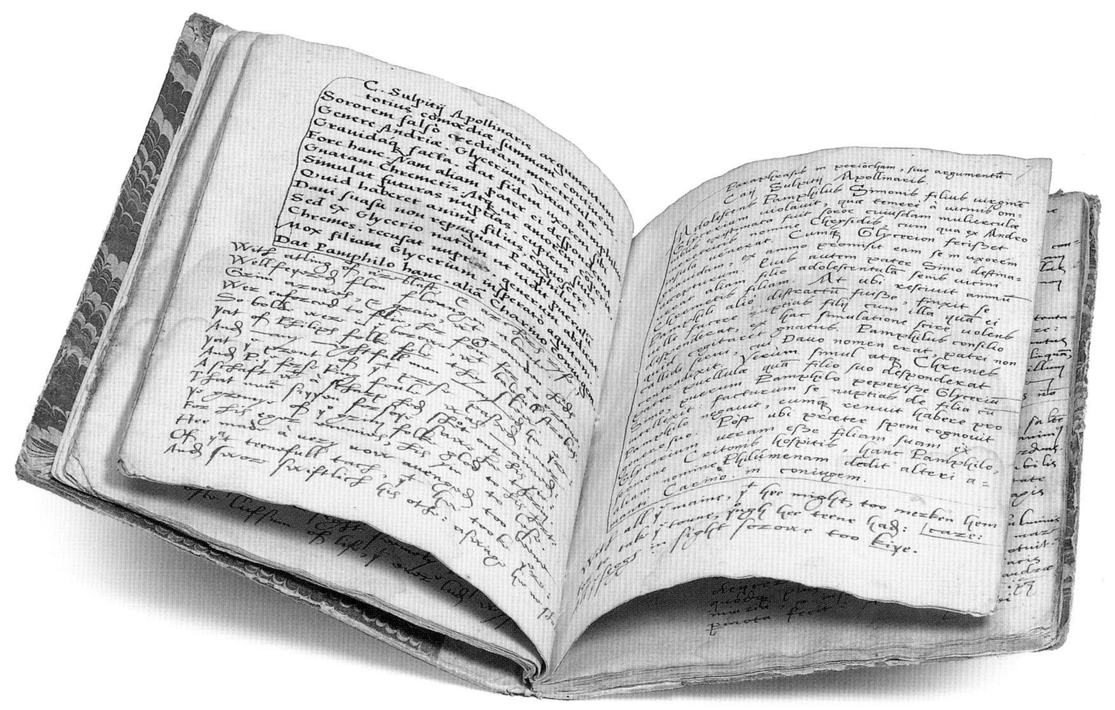

AGO there was a little land, over which ruled a regulus or kinglet, who was called King Peter, although his kingdom was but little. He had four sons whose names were Blaise, Hugh, Gregory, and Ralph. Of these Ralph was the youngest whereas he was but of twenty winters & one; and Blaise was the oldest and had seen thirty winters.

NOW it came to this at the last, that to these young men the kingdom of their father seemed strait; and they longed to see the ways of other men, and to strive for life. For though they were king's sons, they had but little world's wealth; save and except good meat & drink, and enough or too much thereof; up, & the meadows and acres, the woods & the fair streams, & the little hills of Upmeads, for that was the name of their country and the kingdom of King Peter.

So having nought but this little they longed for much; and that the more because, king's sons as they were, they had but scant dominion save over their horses & dogs: for the men of that country were stubborn & sturdy vavassors, and might not away with masterful doings, but were like to pay back a blow with a blow, and a foul word with a buffet. So that, all things considered, it was little wonder if King Peter's sons found themselves straitened in their little land: wherein was no great merchant city; nor no mighty castle, or noble abbey of monks: nought but fair little halls of yeomen, with here & there a franklin's court or a shield-knight's manor-house; with many a goodly church, & whiles a house of good canons, who knew not the road to Rome, or how to find the door

CHAPTER 6

ROMANCE *in the* MODERN WORLD

Alison Wiggins

Today we find romance everywhere. It continues to inspire wonder and amazement and to transport readers to imagined other worlds; at the same time it has retained its function as social commentary and its effect of creating moral and political awareness. The journey of romance from medieval to modern is a story of repeated remakings and reinventions that leaves us asking questions about the relation between literature and life. Although we are only able to track a continuous publication history for *Bevis of Hamtoun*,[1] other romances crossed over into the modern era in something close to their original form. The language of *Roswall and Lillian*, for example, betrays its medieval origins, although the only copies now to survive are much later post-medieval prints, such as *The pleasant History of Roswal and Lillian*, printed probably in Edinburgh *c.*1785 (Bodleian Library, Douce PP 157 (4); fig. 68). These kinds of flimsy, poorly printed little booklets, known as chapbooks, are the cheapest sort of prints, within reach of even those living in the most dire financial straits, whether borrowed, shared or purchased in better times. Chapbooks brought dirt-cheap copies of medieval romance favourites, such as *Guy of Warwick* (fig. 69), *Bevis of Hamtoun* and *Valentine and Orson*, to those whose participation in literary culture was otherwise very limited.

Figure 68. A chapbook edition of *The pleasant History of Roswal and Lillian* (? Edinburgh, *c.* 1785). This copy belonged to the antiquarian and scholar Francis Douce, and is bound into a volume with other fragile chapbooks. Oxford, Bodleian Library, Douce PP 157 (4).

Chapbooks challenge traditional notions of periodization and remind us that cultural artefacts are not hermetically sealed into their originating social milieux. Literary history has a different trajectory at different social levels, and the literature available to the most educated and privileged readers of a particular era was not necessarily simultaneously available to the uneducated or poor. Romances first read by medieval courtiers who valued their detailed attention to the precise intricacies of courtship and chivalry came to be read in the eighteenth and early nineteenth centuries by agricultural and industrial workers living in conditions of miserable poverty and hardship.

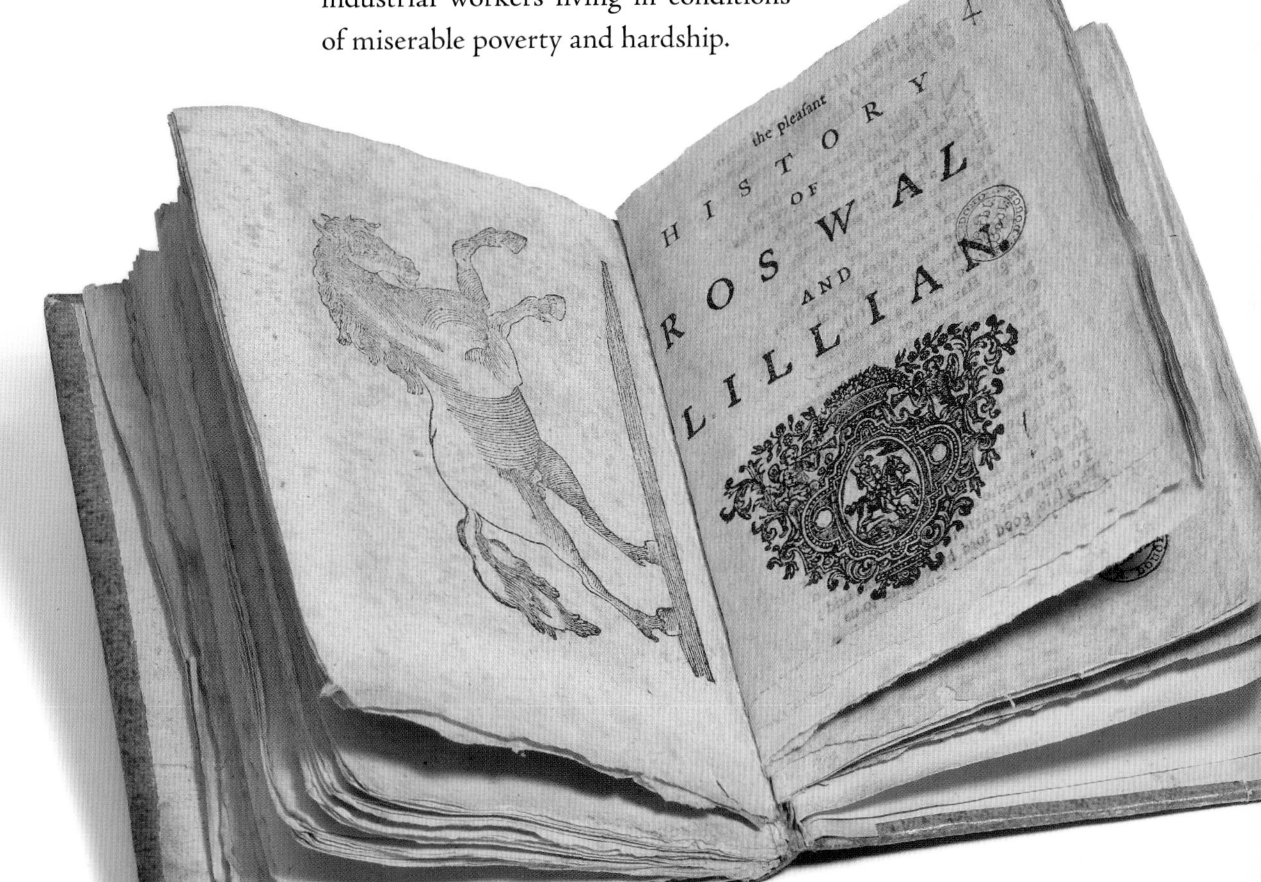

(14)

Chriftians, Guy mantully drew his Sword and the Boar gaping, intending with his dreadful Tufks to devour our noble Champion; but Guy run it down his Throat, and flew the greateft Boar that ever Man beheld.

At Guy's Arrival in England, he immediately repaired to King Athelftone, at York, where the King told Guy of a

mighty Dragon in Northumberland, that deftroyed Men, Women, and Children.—Guy defired a Guide, and went immediately to the Dragon's Cave, when out came the

For these readers romance came to perform new functions, not least the opportunity to enrich the imagination and to experience alternative sets of values and behaviours. In this way, by offering readers another view of reality, romance could stimulate an internal commentary on their own immediate world. Chapbooks therefore show us the place of medieval romance in the struggles and aspirations of ordinary people and their quest for self-improvement. As John Simons has observed, anyone handling these books today 'cannot fail to be moved by the disjunction between their size and fragility and the status they appear to have held in the poor reader's mind'.[2]

As well as being enjoyed by the poorest members of society, chapbooks were read by the children of the gentry and attracted the attention of gentleman collectors, such as poet and novelist Sir Walter Scott (1771–1832). Deeply engaged with oral traditions of romance and balladry, Scott remembered the story of Roswall and Lillian being sung on the streets of Edinburgh. His fascination for romance is well known from novels such as *Ivanhoe* (1820) and *Kenilworth* (1821) and was part of the larger flowering of interest in medieval romance and medievalism throughout the nineteenth century (fig. 70). An insight into Scott's fervent and sometimes

Figure 69 *left.* A chapbook of the popular Guy of Warwick story, printed in Derby in 1796. Objects and sites claimed to be associated with Guy became the centre of an early modern tourist attraction at Warwick Castle; John Evelyn, for example, records a visit there on 3 August 1654 in his Diary. Oxford, Bodleian Library, Douce PP 166, item 18, p. 14.

Figure 70. The Eglinton Tournament of 1839 was one of the most extravagant chivalric events of the nineteenth century, inspired partly by scenes from Walter Scott's *Ivanhoe*. Organized by the Earl of Eglinton and held at his Castle in Ayrshire, the costumed jousts and processions lasted for several days and drew huge crowds, despite some torrential rain. This illustration is taken from a commemorative book, *An Account of the Tournament at Eglinton*, by James Aikman et al. (Edinburgh, 1839). Oxford, Bodleian Library, 2 Δ 301, between pp. 8 and 9.

flamboyant championing of medieval romance is provided for us by the Bodleian Library's inscribed copy of his 1804 edition of *Sir Tristrem* (fig. 71), originally sent by Scott to fellow collector and gentleman-scholar Francis Douce (1757–1834). In an accompanying letter, dated 7 May 1804 and now bound into the volume, Scott explains his objection to the bowdlerization of romance. The copy sent, Scott says, is one of twelve printed uncensored, or, as he puts it, a '"Tristan entier" … thrown off without a castration'. He adds that he would have preferred all copies to be uncastrated and does not believe, as some of his 'respectable friends' do, that 'the coarseness of an ancient romancer is so dangerous to the public as the mongrel & inflammatory sentimen[ts] lately of a modern Novelist'.

The extraordinary achievements and ambitions of nineteenth-century literary figures such as Scott, and antiquarian book collectors like Scott's correspondent Douce, have shaped literary tastes and library holdings and therefore our view of the Middle Ages – Douce's collection of many thousand books is now held by the Bodleian. They have also shaped and influenced the visual arts, not least at Oxford. Two key members of the Pre-Raphaelite and Arts and Crafts movements, William Morris (1834–96) and Edward Burne-Jones (1833–98), met and became lifelong friends whilst students at Oxford. They connected over their shared appreciation of Scott's *Minstrelsy of the Scottish Border* and their fascination with medieval romance, especially Thomas Malory's *Le Morte Darthur* and the Arthurian poetry of Tennyson (fig. 72). The bond between the young artists was strengthened in 1857–59, during a collaborative venture with Dante Gabriel Rossetti (1828–82) and others, painting the new Debating Chamber (now called the Old Library)

Figure 71. Sir Walter Scott's edition of *Sir Tristrem* (Edinburgh, 1804) with his letter to Francis Douce, dated 7 May 1804, tipped in to the binding. Scott edited the romance from the version found in the Auchinleck Manuscript, then part of the Advocates' Library in Edinburgh. Oxford, Bodleian Library, Douce E. 264.

by no means think that the coarseness of an ancient romancer is so dangerous to the public as the mongrel & inflammatory sentimentality of a modern Novelist. By honouring with your acceptance a "*Tristan entier*" you will greatly oblige

Sir
Your most obedient humble Servt

Walter Scott

Edin^r. Castle Street.
May 7 – 1804.

Francis Douce Esq
F. A. S.

Francis Douce Esqr.
F. A. S.
from the Editor.

SIR TRISTREM.

in the Oxford Union building with murals depicting scenes from Arthurian legend. The group failed to prepare the walls properly, and so the murals are in poor condition, but they can still be seen in Oxford today, as can many other Pre-Raphaelite paintings, tapestries, stained glass windows, decorative designs and drawings, such as Burne-Jones's *The Knight's Farewell* (1858) (fig. 73). The Pre-Raphaelites' interests extended to the material book and the revival of neglected crafts of manuscript illumination, calligraphy and long forgotten printing techniques. These activities culminated in the remarkable Kelmscott Press, founded in 1891, from which Morris published several medieval romances as well as his own romance *The Well at the World's End*, illustrated by Burne-Jones (fig. 74). The pages of these books are magical windows onto an imagined medieval past, an idealized world of melancholy beauty and spirituality that seems distant and at the same time vividly alive and real. Their paintings, which often favour the rich primary colours of medieval stained glass, are mesmerizing jewelled boxes that remind us of the powerful and compelling appeal of medieval romance to the visual imagination. For Morris and Burne-Jones romance is an escape to an ethereal sphere that is a corrective to the industrialism and commercialism of their own time. Their medievalism is an expression of their developing socialist philosophy: a belief in the humanizing dignity of creative labour, by contrast with the automatizing effects upon ordinary people of industrial factory work.

Morris's medievalism and fantasy writing were among the inspirations for J.R.R. Tolkien (1892–1973), C.S. Lewis (1886–1945), and their fellow Inklings. As for their Pre-Raphaelite predecessors, Oxford was a place where they explored and were inspired by medi-

Figure 72. Tennyson's Arthurian works, including *The Idylls of the King* and *The Lady of Shalott* inspired many artistic responses. William Holman Hunt (1827–1910) had illustrated the latter with Dante Gabriel Rossetti for an 1857 edition of Tennyson's works. He returned to the theme several times, including in this painting of *c.* 1887–1892, whose rich symbolism conveys a troubling vision of female entrapment and the ambivalent relationship between duty, desire and the creative imagination. Holman Hunt, *The Lady of Shalott*, © Manchester City Art Galleries, 1934.401 (oil on canvas).

ROMAN
QUETE

Figure 73. Edward Burne-Jones's *The Knight's Farewell* (1858) is inspired by the medieval manuscripts and medievalist ideas that he encountered with William Morris after they met as students in Oxford in 1853. The inclusion of a book of the Grail quest connects the picture with a narrative that obsessed the artist throughout his career. © Ashmolean Museum, University of Oxford, WA 1977.34 (pen and ink on vellum).

Figure 74. *pp. 162–3. The well at the world's end (with four pictures designed by sir E. Burne-Jones)* was painstakingly produced by The Kelmscott Press at Hammersmith in 1896. Printed on handmade paper, it uses the Press's own hand-cut and hand-set Chaucer typeface. William Morris's narrative is a fantasy of chivalric quest and adventure drawing on the language and motifs of medieval romance. The start of the book features a wood-engraved illustration with the caption 'Help is to hand in the wood perilous'. Oxford, Bodleian Library, Kelmscott Press d.13, title page.

eval romance. Tolkien and Lewis were among the leading medieval scholars of their day, and from their deep and direct engagement with medieval languages and literature the genre of modern fantasy fiction was invented and has flourished (figs 75–77). Both held a strong commitment to romance as a mode of writing that deserves serious attention; it is well recognized, for example, that Tolkien's fiction is not simply escapist but provides social commentary on his own time and engages with ecological agendas that are well ahead of it. One Oxford student who heard Tolkien lecture in the 1960s was Terry Jones, whose interest in medieval literature has continued as a lifelong passion, perhaps most famously in the 1974 film *Monty Python and The Holy Grail*, which Jones co-directed and which brilliantly parodies the excesses of Arthurian romance (figs 78 and 79). In a recent interview, Jones reflects on his memories of student life at Oxford, where he met Python-to-be Michael Palin: 'I remember J.R.R. Tolkien giving a lecture on *Beowulf* in the Examination Schools. The room was packed. He started off reading with great animation, and then he stopped, pulled out his handkerchief, and – amid a great laugh – put his false teeth in!'[3] This snapshot presents to us Tolkien the great philologist, so absorbed in medieval literature that he forgets his own teeth; a man who never anticipated the astonishing success his fiction would have, nor could have dreamed of the global impact of Peter Jackson's spectacular film adaptations of *The Lord of the Rings* (2001–03).

Medieval romance continues to inspire artists, film-makers, poets, novelists and composers. The rich variety of responses to *Sir Gawain and the Green Knight* includes Iris Murdoch's *The Green Knight* (1993); Harrison Birtwistle's opera *Gawain*, with

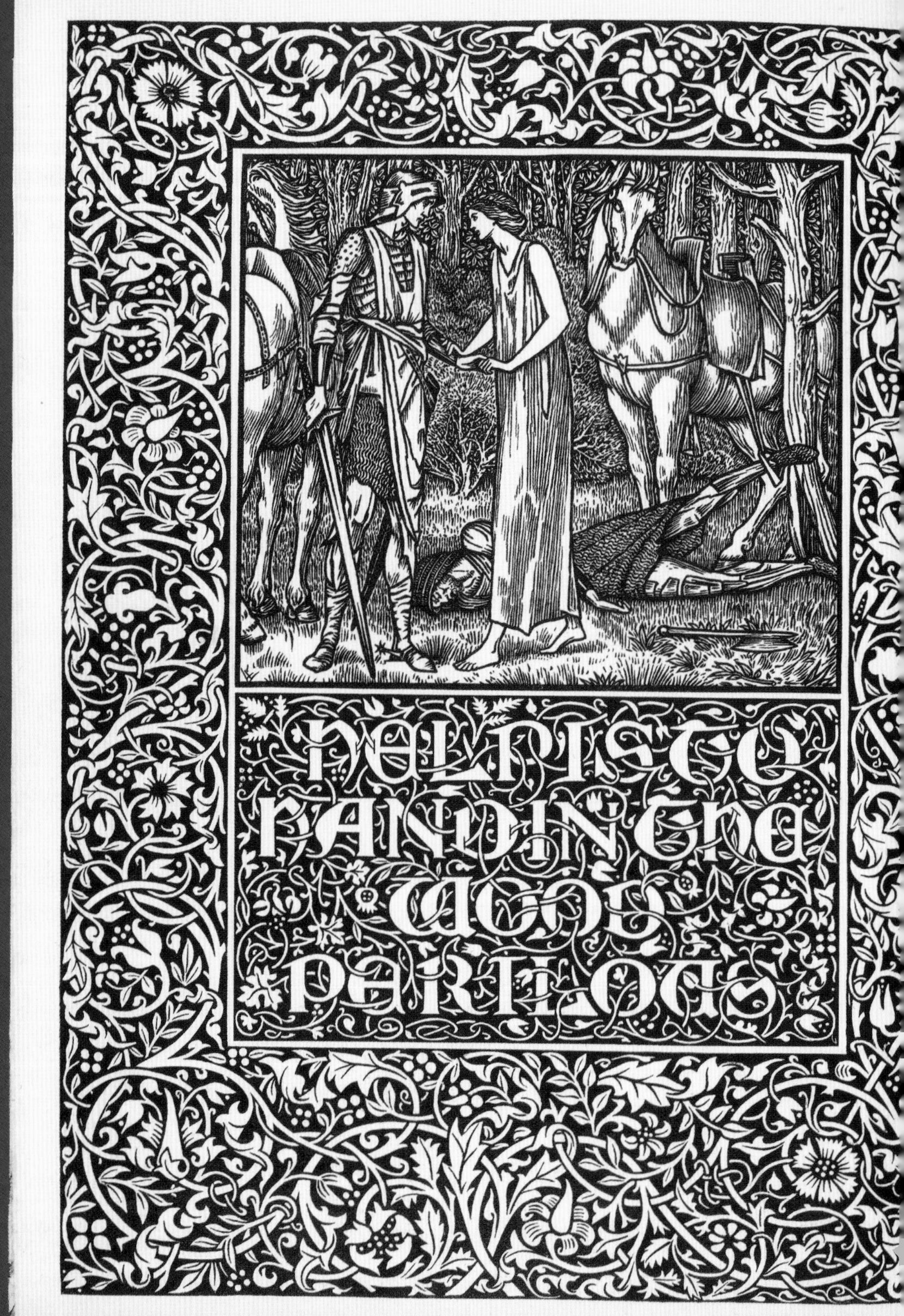
HELP IS TO
HAND IN THE
WOOD
PERILOUS

THE WELL AT THE WORLD'S END
BOOK I. THE ROAD UNTO LOVE

Chapter I. The Sundering of the Ways

LONG AGO there was a little land, over which ruled a regulus or kinglet, who was called King Peter, although his kingdom was but little. He had four sons whose names were Blaise, Hugh, Gregory, and Ralph. Of these Ralph was the youngest whereas he was but of twenty winters & one; and Blaise was the oldest and had seen thirty winters.

NOW it came to this at the last, that to these young men the kingdom of their father seemed strait; and they longed to see the ways of other men, and to strive for life. For though they were king's sons, they had but little world's wealth; save and except good meat & drink, and enough or too much thereof; house-room of the best; fair friends to be merry with, and maidens to kiss, and these also as good as might be; freedom withal to come and go as they would; the heavens above them, the earth to bear them up, & the meadows and acres, the woods & the fair streams, & the little hills of Upmeads, for that was the name of their country and the kingdom of King Peter.

So having nought but this little they longed for much; and that the more because, king's sons as they were, they had but scant dominion save over their horses & dogs: for the men of that country were stubborn & sturdy vavassors, and might not away with masterful doings, but were like to pay back a blow with a blow, and a foul word with a buffet. So that, all things considered, it was little wonder if King Peter's sons found themselves straitened in their little land: wherein was no great merchant city; nor no mighty castle, or noble abbey of monks: nought but fair little halls of yeomen, with here & there a franklin's court or a shield-knight's manor-house; with many a goodly church, & whiles a house of good canons, who knew not the road to Rome, or how to find the door libretto by David Harsent (1991, revised 1994); and Simon Armitage's stunning northern dialect translation (2006).[4] Many of the most successful fantasy and science-fiction creations of the post-Tolkien era take the familiar themes and structures of romance and engage these with current social, political and religious debates and controversies. Among these are Ursula Le Guin's *Earthsea* novels (1968–2001), which critique cultural attitudes to race and gender; Philip Pullman's *His Dark Materials* trilogy (1995–2000), which questions the role of organized religion; and the revived *Battlestar Galactica*'s television space quest (2003–10), which examines post-9/11 politics. Whether their creators acknowledge it or not, we must recognize that medieval romances and manuscripts are a point of origin for all of these, and new examples occasionally come to light even today. One recent discovery came to notice in 1996 as a bundle of manuscript fragments and notes in blue biro all held together with packing tape: a confection nicknamed by its

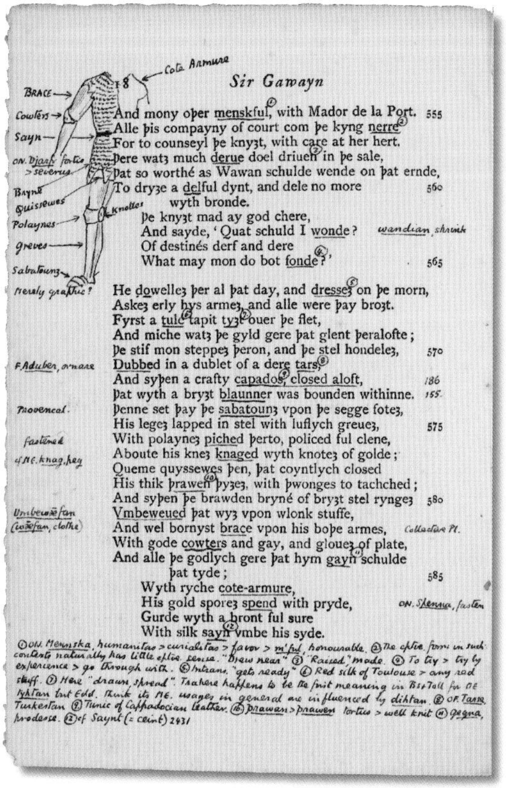

Figure 75 *left.* J.R.R. Tolkien and E.V. Gordon's 1925 edition of *Sir Gawain and the Green Knight* became the standard text, stimulating new study and analysis. Poet Simon Armitage first came to the poem in his twenties through this edition, and years later was prompted to produce his translation when his wife's 'dog-eared copy' fell open and he caught sight of the word 'wodwo'. The copy shown here belonged to C.S. Lewis, whose annotations reveal his fastidious attention to the details of the poem. Oxford, Bodleian Library, Arch. H e.55, p. 18. © The J.R.R. Tolkien Copyright Trust 2012.

Figure 76. This holograph draft page from *The Two Towers* features J.R.R. Tolkien's drawing of Shelob's Lair, with the text wrapping around it. Tolkien initially drafted the text in pencil, before writing over it in pen. Oxford, Bodleian Library, MS Tolkien drawings 81 (pencil, black ink and red crayon). © The J.R.R. Tolkien Copyright Trust 1976, 1979, 1995.

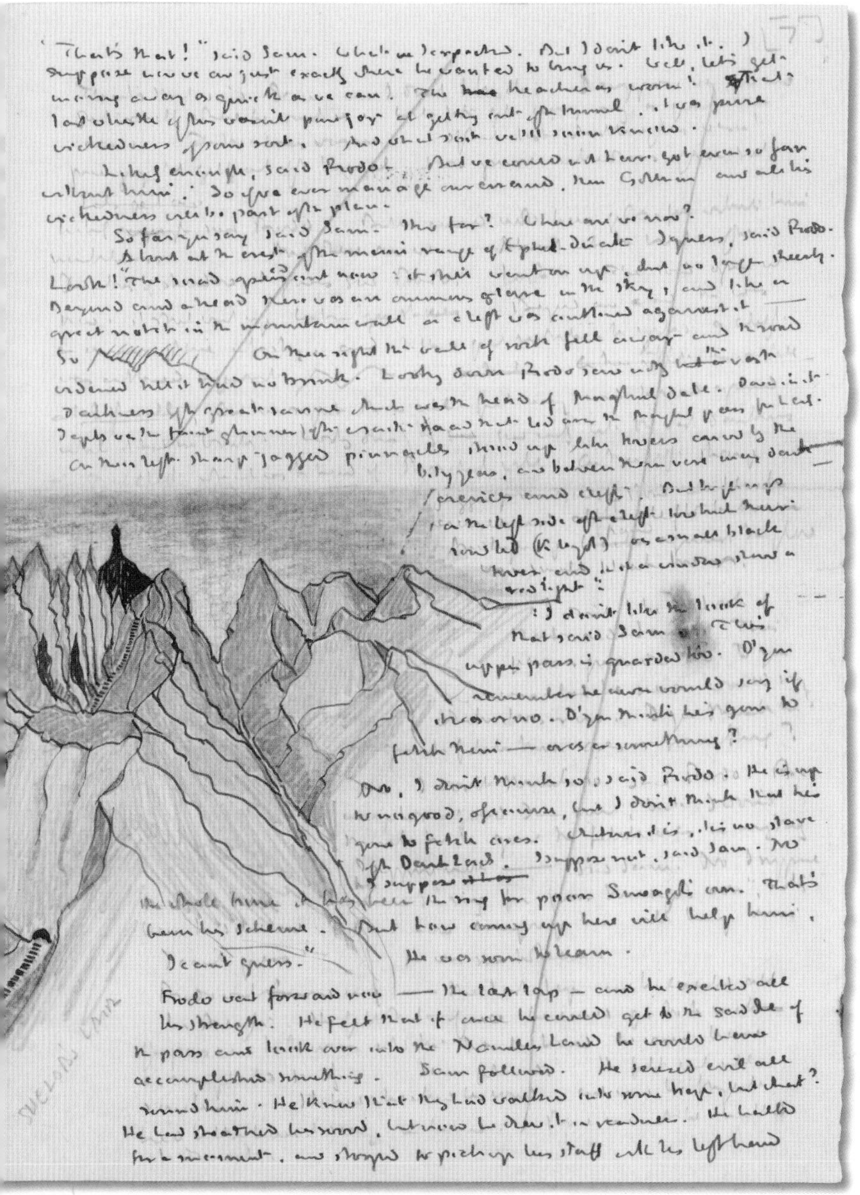

owner a 'poetry pasty' (Bodleian MS Eng. poet. d. 208; fig. 80).[5] Archivists are perpetually engaged with the question of how best to preserve and present original books containing medieval romance, such as this one, for future generations. It is a question which runs parallel to those asked by scholarly editors of romance, whether in print or online. As the web opens up medieval romance to new readers, rare and precious manuscripts can now be viewed on-screen in all corners of the world. From *Le Morte Darthur* to *The Dark is Rising*, from *Sir Tristrem* to Sir Terry Pratchett, and from the vaults of the Bodleian Library to the computer screen, the story of romance continues into the twenty-first century.

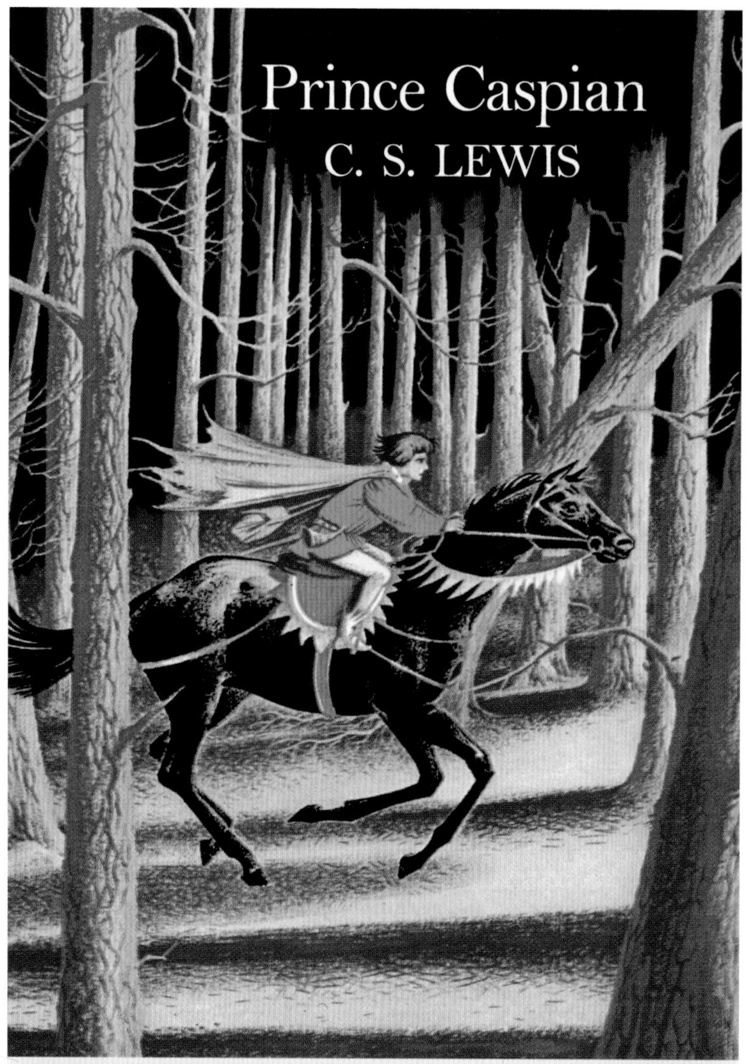

Prince Caspian
C. S. LEWIS
The Chronicles of Narnia
FULL-COLOUR COLLECTOR'S EDITION

Figure 77 *left.* The books of Tolkien and C.S. Lewis are inextricably linked with the artwork of Pauline Baynes (1922–2008). Her drawings reinterpreting marginal images from the medieval Luttrell Psalter brought her to Tolkien's attention. She illustrated numerous books for Tolkien, alongside many other projects, including nearly 600 illustrations for Grant Uden's *A Dictionary of Chivalry* (1968). Baynes later recalled writing in her diary: 'Met C S Lewis. Went home. Made rock cakes.' Her Narnia illustrations are an iconic part of the books' success, as with this cover image from *Prince Caspian*. Jacket by Pauline Baynes © C.S. Lewis Pte. Ltd. 1951. Reprinted by permission. Image courtesy of HarperCollins.

Figure 78. Terry Jones's copy of the shooting script for *Monty Python and the Holy Grail* is full of notes, drawings and revisions to the film's dialogue. The famous Black Knight scene sends up the extravagant rhetoric of *chanson*-style violence favoured by popular romance. Similar delight is found in a particularly Pythonesque moment in the *Stanzaic Guy of Warwick*. When Guy cuts off the right arm of his gigantic opponent, Amoraunt grabs a sword with his left hand and revives his attack. Guy then cuts off Amoraunt's remaining hand,

6.

3. DAY. EXTERIOR. FOREST

MIX THROUGH TO FOREST GLADE. ARTHUR AND PATSY PROCEEDING THROUGH IT. THEY REACH THE EDGE OF IT AND AS THEY DO THEY OBSERVE BY A BRIDGE CROSSING A RIVER A TREMENDOUS FIGHT WHICH IS REACHING ITS END. THIS TAKES PLACE BETWEEN A HUGE KNIGHT IN BLACK ARMOUR AND A PRETTY IMPRESSIVE LOOKING ONE THOUGH SLIGHTLY SMALLER IN GREEN ARMOUR. THE BLACK KNIGHT AVOIDS A BLOW AND RUNS HIS OPPONENT THROUGH. THE GREEN KNIGHT COLLAPSES IN DEATH THROES. THE BLACK KNIGHT IMMEDIATELY TAKES UP A POSITION BARRING THE BRIDGE. ARTHUR MAKES AS THOUGH TO SPUR HIS HORSE FORWARD AND FOLLOWED CLOSELY BY PATSY TROTS ACROSS THE OPEN GROUND BETWEEN THE EDGE OF THE GLADE AND THE BRIDGE. POSS ASKS BLACK KNIGHT TO JOIN HIM

A: ~~Let me pass good Sir Knight.~~

K: None shall pass.

A: I have no quarrel with you brave Sir Knight, but I must cross this bridge.

K: Then you shall die.

A: I command you, as King of the Britons to stand aside.

K: I move for no man.

A: So be it.

ARTHUR DRAWS HIS SWORD AND APPROACHES THE BLACK KNIGHT. A FURIOUS FIGHT NOW STARTS LASTING ABOUT FIFTEEN SECONDS AT WHICH POINT ARTHUR DELIVERS A MIGHTY BLOW WHICH COMPLETELY SEVERS THE BLACK KNIGHT'S LEFT ARM AT THE SHOULDER. ARTHUR STEPS BACK TRIUMPHANTLY.

A: Now stand aside worthy adversary.

K: (GLANCING AT SHOULDER) Tis just a scratch.

A: A scratch. Your arm's off.

K: No it isn't.

A: What's that then? (POINTING TO ARM ON GROUND)

K: I've had worse.

A: You're a liar.

K: Come on you pansy.

at which 'on Sir Guii he lepe with alle his might / That almast he had feld him doun right' (lines 1585–6: leaps on top of Guy with his whole body weight, almost managing to floor him).

Monty Python and the Holy Grail, unpublished second draft of screenplay, by John Cleese, Graham Chapman, Terry Gilliam, Eric Idle, Terry Jones and Michael Palin (1973), fol. 6r. Image courtesy of Terry Jones.

Figure 79. 'All right, we'll call it a draw' says the now limbless Black Knight (John Cleese), while King Arthur (Graham Chapman) looks on incredulously. Cleese played the Black Knight while he had both legs; when one was cut off by Arthur, a one-legged silversmith named Richard Burton stepped in, to avoid Cleese having to strap one leg and balance on the other. Once down to his torso, Cleese took over again. In 2005 the film's success was continued through its adaptation into the hit musical *Spamalot*. *Monty Python and the Holy Grail* (1975). © Python (Monty) Pictures Ltd.

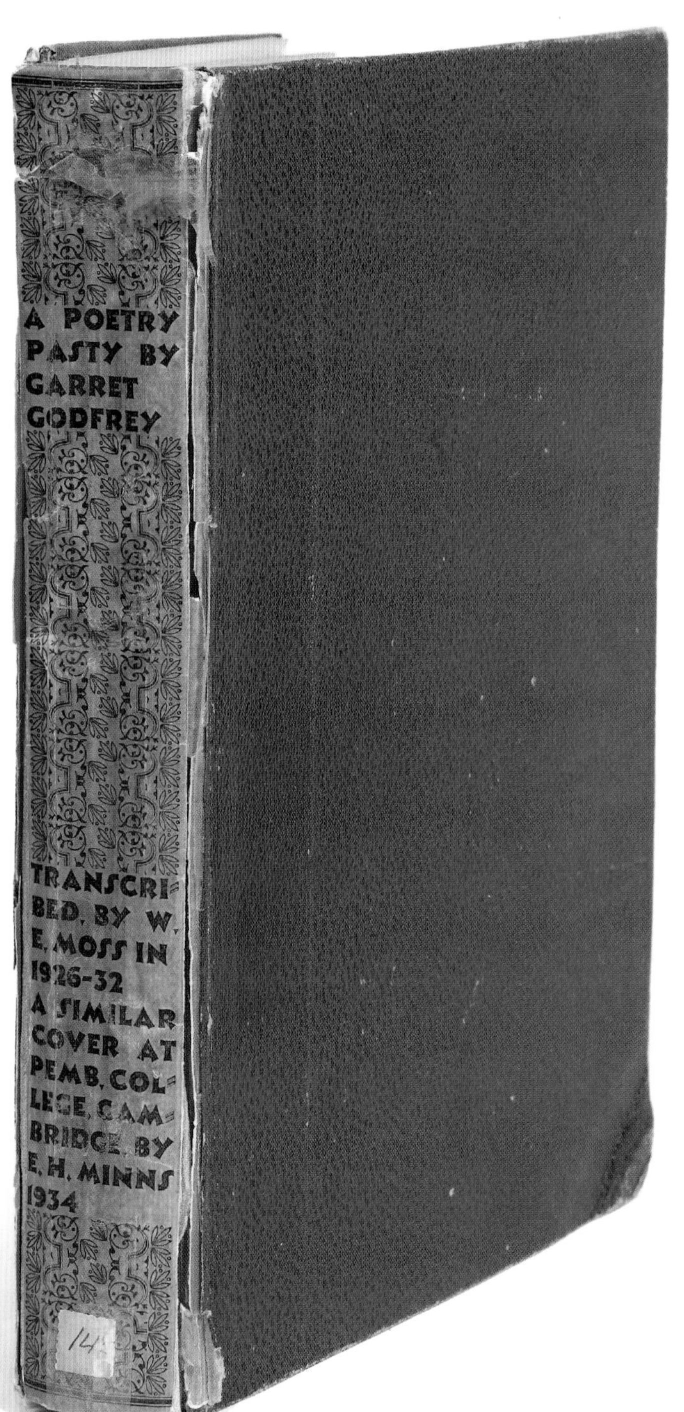

Figure 80. 'A poetry pasty by Garret Godfrey, Transcribed by Colonel W. E. Moss in 1926–32'. The book and its accompanying envelope contain numerous notes, papers and letters of Colonel Moss. These record his attempts to make sense of the 'pasty' by identifying its romance texts and by trying to figure out how the manuscript fragments fit together. Oxford, Bodleian Library, MS Eng. poet. d. 208.

NOTES

Chapter 1

1. *Sir Gawain and the Green Knight*, lines 93–5, quoted from *The Poems of the Pearl Manuscript*, ed. Malcolm Andrew and Ronald Waldron, rev. edn (Exeter, 2007). Translations are my own unless otherwise specified.
2. 'The Knight Sets Forth', in Eric Auerbach, *Mimesis: The Representation of Reality in Western Literature*, trans. Willard Trask (1953; repr. Princeton NJ, 2003), pp. 123–42. Auerbach famously wrote this book in Istanbul between 1942 and 1945, a Jewish exile from Nazi Germany.
3. Sir Thomas Malory, *Works*, ed. Eugène Vinaver, 2nd edn (Oxford, 1971), p. xv.
4. See Jacques Derrida, 'The Law of Genre', trans. Avital Ronell, *Critical Inquiry* 7 (1980), pp. 55–81.
5. Geoffrey Chaucer, *The Canterbury Tales*, in *The Riverside Chaucer*, ed. Larry D. Benson (Oxford, 1988), Fragment I, lines 3110–13.
6. Ibid., Fragment VII, lines 925, 930.
7. *The Paston Letters*, ed. Norman Davis (Oxford, 1999), quoting p. 166. See G.A. Lester, *John Paston's 'Grete Boke': A Descriptive Catalogue, with an Introduction, of British Library MS Lansdowne 285* (Cambridge, 1984).
8. See James A. Rushing, 'Adventure in the Service of Love: Yvain on a Fourteenth-Century Panel', *Zeitschrift für Kunstgeschichte* 61 (1998), pp. 55–65; and *Images in Ivory: Precious Objects of the Gothic Age*, ed. Peter Barnet (Princeton NJ, 1997). A website devoted to Gothic ivories is now accessible at www.gothicivories.courtauld.ac.uk.
9. See Chrétien de Troyes, *Arthurian Romances*, trans. D.D.R. Owen (London, 1987).
10. 'Nere theos ilke leafdi of uveles cunnes cunde, yef ha over alle thing ne luvede him her-efter?'; *Ancrene Wisse*, ed. Robert Hasenfratz (Kalamazoo MI, 2000), p. 380: www.lib.rochester.edu/camelot/teams/tmsmenu.htm#menu. Many romances are also available online in this series. See too *Ancrene Wisse; Guide for Anchoresses*, trans. Bella Millett (Exeter, 2009).
11. C-text VII. lines 11–12, quoting MS Douce 104, fol. 30v; see *Piers Plowman: A New Annotated Edition of the C-text*, ed. Derek Pearsall (Exeter, 2008).
12. John Gower, *Confessio amantis*, ed. Russell A. Peck, 2 vols (Kalamazoo MI, 2000–2003; 2nd edn 2006): www.lib.rochester.edu/camelot/teams/rpca1.htm. See Jeremy Dimmick, '"Redinge of Romance" in Gower's *Confessio Amantis*', in *Tradition and Transformation in Medieval Romance*, ed. Rosalind Field (Cambridge, 1999), pp. 125–37.
13. *Pericles*, I.i. 1–10, in *The Riverside Shakespeare*, ed. G. Blakemore Evans, rev. edn (Boston MA, 1997), p. 1531.

Chapter 2

1. Wace, *Roman de Rou*, ed. A.J. Holden (Paris, 1971), lines 8013–18; *The History of the Norman People*, trans. Glyn S. Burgess (Woodbridge, 2004), p. 181.
2. *La Chanson de Roland*, ed. Ian Short (Paris, 1990), lines 1761–4.
3. *The Romance of Horn*, ed. Mildred K. Pope, 2 vols, Anglo-Norman Text Society 9–10, 12–13 (1955–64), lines 5231–3.
4. *King Horn*, ed. Ronald D. Herzman et al. (Kalamazoo MI, 1999), lines 1216–22: www.lib.rochester.edu/camelot/teams/hornint.htm.
5. *The Laud Troy Book*, ed. J. Ernst Wülfing, EETS o.s. 121–2 (London, 1902), lines 13–19.
6. *Sir Gawain and the Green Knight*, in *Poems of the Pearl Manuscript*, ed. Malcolm Andrew and Ronald Waldron, rev. edn (Exeter, 2007), lines 13–19.
7. *Troilus and Criseyde*, II. 22–6, in *The Riverside Chaucer*, ed. Larry D. Benson (Oxford, 1988).
8. See Julia Boffey, 'Bodleian Library, MS Arch. Selden B. 24 and Definitions of the "Household Book"', in *The English Medieval Book: Studies in Memory of Jeremy Griffiths*, ed. A.S.G. Edwards et al. (London, 2000), pp. 125–34.
9. Nicola McDonald, 'Eating People and the Alimentary Logic of *Richard Coeur de Lion*', in Nicola McDonald, ed., *Pulp Fictions of Medieval England: Essays in Popular Romance* (Manchester, 2004), pp. 124–50.
10. Auchinleck Manuscript text, lines 579–82, http://auchinleck.nls.uk/mss/tars.html.
11. See Daniel Huws, *Medieval Welsh Manuscripts* (Cardiff, 2000).
12. *Awntyrs off Arthur*, in *Sir Gawain: Eleven Romances and Tales*, ed. Thomas Hahn (Kalamazoo MI, 1995), www.lib.rochester.edu/camelot/teams/awnfrm.htm.
13. *Alexander and Dindimus*, ed. Walter W. Skeat, EETS e.s. 31 (London, 1878), lines 568–72.

Chapter 3

1. *Havelok*, ed. G.V. Smithers (Oxford, 1987).
2. *Floire et Blancheflor*, ed. Margaret Pelan, 2nd edn (Paris, 1956). See Melissa Furrow, *Expectations of Romance: The Reception of a Genre in Medieval England* (Cambridge, 2009) for the 'persistent engagement with romances' (p. 223) both by monastic orders and secular clergy.
3. See Richard Beadle, 'Middle English Texts and their Transmission, 1350–1500: Some Geographical Criteria', in Margaret Laing and Keith Williamson, eds, *Speaking in Our Tongues: Medieval Dialectology and Related Disciplines* (Cambridge, 1994), pp. 69–91.
4. See Ralph Hanna, *London Literature, 1300–1380* (Cambridge, 2005).
5. See Richard Beadle, 'Prologomena to a Literary Geography of Later Medieval Norfolk', in Felicity Riddy, ed., *Regionalism in Late Medieval Manuscripts and Texts* (Cambridge, 1991), pp. 89–108.
6. See A.S.G. Edwards, 'The Contexts of the Vernon Romances', in Derek Pearsall, ed., *Studies in the Vernon Manuscript* (Cambridge, 1990), pp. 159–70.
7. Mary J. Carruthers, *The Book of Memory: A Study of Memory in Medieval Culture* (Cambridge, 1992), pp. 246–7 (2nd edn 2008); discussed by Phillipa Hardman, 'Evidence of Readership in Fifteenth-Century Household Miscellanies', *Poetica* 60 (2003), pp. 15–30.
8. Here summarising the detailed discussion of this book (including re-consideration of Lister Mather's description of it as 'a sort of family book') in Carole M. Meale, 'The Politics of Book Ownership: The Hopton Family and Bodleian Library, Digby MS 185', in Felicity Riddy, ed., *Prestige, Authority and Power in Late Medieval Manuscripts and Texts* (Woodbridge, 2000), pp. 103–31.
9. *Reinbrun*, line 144, in *The Auchinleck Manuscript*, ed. David Burnley and Alison Wiggins, National Library of Scotland Digital Library, 2003, www.nls.uk/auchinleck; accessed 2 March 2011.
10. 'The Fair Maid of Ribblesdale', lines 37–9, in *The Harley Lyrics*, ed. G.L. Brook (Manchester, 1948), reading 'romaunz' for Brook's 'romaunȝ'.
11. Geoffrey Chaucer, *The Canterbury Tales*, in *The Riverside Chaucer*, ed. Larry D. Benson (Oxford, 1988), VII. 3211–13.
12. For a detailed discussion of Isabel Lyston and her will, see Carole M. Meale, '"Gode men / Wives, maydnes and alle men": Romance and its Audience', in Carole M. Meale, *Readings in Medieval Romance* (Cambridge, 1994), pp. 208–25.
13. See further Sarah Kay, 'Analytical Survey 3: The New Philology', *New Medieval Literatures* 3 (2000), pp. 295–326, esp. p. 317.

Chapter 4

1. *Isumbras* and *Gowther* are included in *Six Middle English Romances*, ed. Maldwyn Mills (London, 1973); *Amis and Amiloun* in *Of Love and Chivalry*, ed. Jennifer Fellows (London, 1993). All are edited in the online TEAMS series.
2. See Melissa Furrow, *Expectations of Romance: The Reception of a Genre in Medieval England* (Cambridge, 2009), pp. 6–12. Many of the tiles are now in the British Museum.
3. Dante Alighieri, *The Divine Comedy: Inferno*, ed. and trans. Charles S. Singleton (Princeton NJ, 1970), V. 130–38.
4. See Henrike Manuwald and Nick Humphrey, 'A Painted Casket in the Victoria and Albert Museum, London', *Antiquaries Journal* 90 (2010), pp. 235–60.
5. *Les Fragments du 'Roman de Tristan'*, ed. Bartina H. Wind (Leiden, 1950), p. 89, lines 649–56; see also Thomas, *Tristan*, in Gottfried von Strassburg, *Tristan*, trans. A.T. Hatto (Harmondsworth, 1960).
6. *The Anglo-Norman 'Folie Tristan'*, ed. Ian Short, Anglo-Norman Text Society (London, 1993), lines 175–6; 181–2; *The Birth of Romance: An Anthology*, trans. Judith Weiss (London, 1992), p. 124.
7. *Folie Tristan*, Line 917; *The Birth of Romance*, p. 138.
8. MS Ashmole 61 text, lines 66–8, 70, in *Sir Orfeo*, ed. A.J. Bliss, 2nd edn (Oxford, 1966).
9. *Owein*, ed. R.L. Thomson (Dublin, 1968), p. 21; *The Mabinogion*, trans. Sioned Davies (Oxford, 2007), p. 131.
10. *Eger and Grime*, ed. James Ralston Caldwell (Cambridge MA, 1933); Percy Folio version, lines 1104–8.
11. See P.D.A. Harvey, *Mappa Mundi: The Hereford World Map*, 2nd edn (Hereford, 2002).
12. Printed in *Sir Gawain: Eleven Romances and Tales*, ed. Thomas Hahn (Kalamazoo MI, 1995), lines 422–4, www.lib.rochester.edu/Camelot/teams/ragnfrm.htm.
13. See Julia Boffey and Carol M. Meale, 'Selecting the Text: Rawlinson C.86 and some Other Books for London Readers', in Felicity Riddy, ed., *Regionalism in Late Medieval Manuscripts and Texts* (Cambridge, 1991), pp. 143–69.
14. See Seth Lerer, *Courtly Letters in the Age of Henry VIII: Literary Culture and the Arts of Deceit* (Cambridge, 1997).
15. *Morte Darthur*, in Sir Thomas Malory, *Works*, ed. Eugène Vinaver, 2nd edn (Oxford, 1971), p. 725.

Chapter 5

1. For further information about Caxton and the first printed books in English, see the British Library's online edition of 'Caxton's Chaucer': www.bl.uk/treasures/caxton/firstbook.html.
2. See further Jennifer Fellows, 'Printed Romance in the Sixteenth Century', in Raluca L. Radulescu and Cory James Rushton, eds, *A Companion to Medieval Popular Romance* (Cambridge, 2009), pp. 67–78.
3. See John Finlayson, 'Legendary Ancestors and the Expansion of Romance in *Richard*

Coeur de Lyon', *English Studies* 79 (1998), pp. 299–308.

4. For further information, especially on de Worde's printing of *Richard Coeur de Lyon* and on Buckingham's library, see Carole M. Meale, 'Caxton, de Worde, and the Publication of Romance in Late Medieval England', *The Library*, sixth series 14 (1992), pp. 297–8.
5. For example, Bodleian Library MS Douce 236, discussed in Chapter 3.
6. For a full account, see Julia Boffey and Carol M. Meale, 'Selecting the Text: Rawlinson C. 86 and Some Other Books for London Readers', in Felicity Riddy, ed., *Regionalism in Late Medieval Manuscripts and Texts* (Cambridge, 1991), pp. 143–69.
7. This suggestion is made by Meale in '"Prenes: engre": An Early Sixteenth-century Presentation Copy of *The Erle of Tolous*', in Jennifer Fellows et al., eds, *Romance Reading on the Book: Essays on Medieval Narrative Presented to Maldwyn Mills* (Cardiff, 1996), pp. 221–36, at p. 232, to which I am indebted.
8. For the identification of Bannister, see M.C. Seymour, 'MSS Douce 261 and Egerton 3132A and Edward Banyster', *Bodleian Library Record* 10 (1980), pp. 162–5; and H.R. Woudhuysen, *Sir Philip Sidney and the Circulation of Manuscripts 1558–1640* (Oxford, 1996), pp. 242–5. For further discussion and facsimile images, see Maldwyn Mills, 'EB and his Two Books: Visual Impact and the Power of Meaningful Suggestion. "Reading" the Illustrations in MSS Douce 261 and Egerton 3132A', in Stephen Kelly and John J. Thompson, eds, *Imagining the Book* (Turnhout, 2005), pp. 173–91.
9. See Helen Cooper, *The English Romance in Time: Transforming Motifs from Geoffrey of Monmouth to the Death of Shakespeare* (Oxford, 2004), p. 38. Cooper provides a detailed summary overview of romance in the post-medieval period (at pp. 34–40), from which this chapter has benefited throughout.
10. Fellows, 'Printed Romance', p. 68.
11. Tessa Watt, *Cheap Print and Popular Piety, 1550–1640* (Cambridge, 1993), p. 268. For an edition, see *Robert Langham, A Letter*, ed. R.J.P. Kuin (Leiden, 1983).
12. Cooper, *The English Romance in Time*, p. 36.
13. George Puttenham, 'The Art of English Poesy (1589)', in *Sidney's 'The Defence of Poesy' and Selected Renaissance Literary Criticism*, ed. Gavin Alexander (London, 2004), p. 124.
14. Watt, *Cheap Print*, p. 14, note 17.
15. 'The Anatomie of Absvrditie', in *The Works of Thomas Nashe*, ed. R.B. McKerrow; corrected edn ed. F.P. Wilson, 5 vols (Oxford, 1958), I. 26.
16. On Spenser's engagement with medieval romance, see Andrew King, *The Faerie Queene and Middle English Romance: The Matter of Just Memory* (Oxford, 2000), as well as his essays '*Guy of Warwick* and *The Faerie Queene*, Book II: Chivalry Through the Ages', in Alison Wiggins and Rosalind Field, eds, *Guy of Warwick: Icon and Ancestor*, (Woodbridge, 2007), pp. 169–84; and 'Sidney and Spenser', in *A Companion to Romance From Classical to Contemporary*, ed. Corinne Saunders (Oxford, 2004), pp. 140–59.
17. See the *Oxford Dictionary of National Biography* online articles for Sir Thomas Hoby, Margaret Hoby, Elizabeth Cooke Hoby and Tobie Matthew, at www.oxforddnb.com.
18. For an introduction to these plays, see *Shakespeare's Romances*, ed. Alison Thorne (Basingstoke, 2003).
19. For further details and discussion of these texts, see Helen Cooper, 'Guy as Early Modern English Hero', in *Guy of Warwick*, ed. Wiggins and Field, pp. 185–99.

Chapter 6

1. See Jennifer Fellows, 'The Middle English and Renaissance *Bevis*: A Textual Survey', in *Sir Bevis of Hampton in Literary Tradition*, ed. Jennifer Fellows and Ivana Djordjević (Cambridge, 2008), pp. 80–113.
2. *Guy of Warwick and Other Chapbook Romances*, ed. John Simons (Exeter, 1998), p. 2; this chapter has benefited from the assessment of chapbooks in Simons's Introduction.
3. 'A Python's Progress', *Oxford Today*, vol. 22, no. 2 (Hilary Term 2010), www.oxfordtoday.ox.ac.uk/2009-10/v22n2/06.shtml; accessed 14 November 2010.
4. Simon Armitage discusses his influences and inspirations in 'The Knight's Tale', *Guardian*, 16 December 2006, www.guardian.co.uk/books/2006/dec/16/poetry.simonarmitage; accessed 14 November 2010.
5. See Ralph Hanna, 'Unnoticed Middle English Romance Fragments in the Bodleian Library: MS Eng. poet. d. 208', *The Library* 21 (1999), pp. 305–20.

FURTHER READING

Chapter 1

Derek Brewer, *Symbolic Stories: Traditional Narratives of the Family Drama in English Literature* (Harlow, 1980).

Melissa Furrow, *Expectations of Romance: The Reception of a Genre in Medieval England* (Cambridge, 2009).

The Cambridge Companion to Medieval French Literature, ed. Simon Gaunt and Sarah Kay (Cambridge, 2008).

Nicola McDonald, ed., *Pulp Fictions of Medieval England: Essays in Popular Romance* (Manchester, 2004).

Derek Pearsall, *Arthurian Romance: A Short Introduction* (Oxford, 2003).

Ad Putter and Jane Gilbert, eds, *The Spirit of Medieval English Popular Romance* (Harlow, 2000).

Raluca L. Radulescu and Cory James Rushton, eds, *A Companion to Medieval Popular Romance* (Cambridge, 2009).

Chapter 2

Firuza Abdullaeva and Charles Melville, *The Persian Book of Kings: Ibrahim Sultan's 'Shahnama'* (Oxford, 2008); see also http://shahnama.caret.cam.ac.uk/new/jnama/page.

The Birth of Romance: An Anthology, trans. Judith Weiss (London, 1992).

Susan Crane, *Insular Romance: Politics, Faith, and Culture in Anglo-Norman and Middle English Literature* (Berkeley CA, 1986).

Mark Cruse, *Illuminating the 'Roman d'Alexandre': Oxford, Bodleian Library, MS Bodley 264; The Manuscript as Monument* (Cambridge, 2011).

Geraldine Heng, *Empire of Magic: Medieval Romance and the Politics of Cultural Fantasy* (New York, 2003).

Patricia Clare Ingham, *Sovereign Fantasies: Arthurian Romance and the Making of Britain* (Philadelphia PA, 2001).

Sarah Kay, *The Chansons de Geste in the Age of Romance: Political Fictions* (Oxford, 1995).

Donald Maddox and Sara Sturm-Maddox, eds, *The Medieval French Alexander* (Albany NY, 2002).

Richard Stoneman, *Alexander the Great: A Life in Legend* (New Haven CT, 2008).

Chapter 3

The Auchinleck Manuscript, ed. David Burnley and Alison Wiggins, National Library of Scotland Digital Library, 2003, www.nls.uk/auchinleck; accessed 14 November 2010.

Alexandra Gillespie and Daniel Wakelin, eds, *The Production of Books in England, 1350–1500* (Cambridge, 2011).

Gisela Guddat-Figge, *Catalogue of the Manuscripts Containing Middle English Romances* (Munich, 1976).

Carole M. Meale, ed., *Readings in Medieval English Romance* (Cambridge, 1994).

Felicity Riddy, ed., *Prestige, Authority and Power in Late Medieval Manuscripts and Texts* (Woodbridge, 2000).

A Facsimile Edition of the Vernon Manuscript: Oxford, Bodleian Library MS Eng. poet. a. 1, ed. Wendy Scase (Oxford, 2011).

Codex Ashmole 61: A Compilation of Popular Middle English Verse, ed. George Shuffelton (Kalamazoo MI, 2008), www.lib.rochester.edu/camelot/teams/sgas.htm; accessed 14 November 2010.

Chapter 4

Michael Camille, *The Medieval Art of Love* (London, 1998).

Marian Campbell, *Medieval Jewellery in Europe, 1100–1500* (London, 2009).

Jeffrey Jerome Cohen, *Of Giants: Sex, Monsters, and the Middle Ages* (Minneapolis MN, 1996).

Carol Dover, ed., *A Companion to the Lancelot–Grail Cycle* (Woodbridge, 2003).

John Block Friedman, *The Monstrous Races in Medieval Art and Thought* (Syracuse NY, 2000).

Simon Gaunt, *Gender and Genre in Medieval French Literature* (Cambridge, 1995).
Joan Tasker Grimbert, ed., *Tristan and Isolde: A Casebook* (London, 2002).
Jill Mann, *Feminizing Chaucer* (Cambridge, 2002).
A.C. Spearing, *The Medieval Poet as Voyeur: Looking and Listening in Medieval Love-Narratives* (Cambridge, 1993).
Barry Windeatt, *Troilus and Criseyde*, Oxford Guides to Chaucer (Oxford, 1992).

Chapter 5

Helen Cooper, *The English Romance in Time: Transforming Motifs from Geoffrey of Monmouth to the Death of Shakespeare* (Oxford, 2004).
Jennifer Fellows and Ivana Djordjević, eds, *Sir Bevis of Hampton in Literary Tradition* (Woodbridge, 2008).
Andrew King, *The Faerie Queene and Middle English Romance: The Matter of Just Memory* (Oxford, 2000).
John N. King, ed., *Tudor Books and Readers: Materiality and the Construction of Meaning* (Cambridge, 2010).
The Malory Project, directed by Takako Kato and designed by Nick Hayward, 2006, www.maloryproject.com; accessed 14 November 2010.
Carole M. Meale, 'Caxton, de Worde, and the Publication of Romance in Late Medieval England', *The Library*, sixth series 14 (1992), pp. 283–98.
Tessa Watt, *Cheap Print and Popular Piety, 1550–1640* (Cambridge, 1993).
Alison Wiggins and Rosalind Field, eds, *Guy of Warwick: Icon and Ancestor* (Woodbridge, 2007).

Chapter 6

Michael Alexander, *Medievalism: The Middle Ages in Modern England* (New Haven CT, 2007).
Mark Girouard, *The Return to Camelot: Chivalry and the English Gentleman* (New Haven CT, 1981).
The Rossetti Archive, ed. Jerome McGann, University of Virginia, fourth instalment, www.rossettiarchive.org; accessed 14 November 2010.
Corinne Saunders, ed., *A Companion to Romance From Classical to Contemporary* (Oxford, 2004).
Guy of Warwick and other Chapbook Romances: Six Tales from the Popular Literature of pre-Industrial England, ed. John Simons (Exeter, 1998).
Margaret Spufford, *Small Books and Pleasant Histories: Popular Fiction and its Readership in Seventeenth-Century England* (Cambridge, 1985).
Monty Python's Spamalot, www.montypythonsspamalot.com; accessed 14 November 2010.
Morris Online Edition, with turning-the-pages editions of The Kelmscott Press *The Well at the World's End* and *Of the Friendship of Amis and Amile*, University of Iowa Libraries, http://morrisedition.lib.uiowa.edu; accessed 14 November 2010.
Walter Scott Digital Archive, Edinburgh University Library, www.walterscott.lib.ed.ac.uk; accessed 14 November 2010.

INDEX

Note: specific manuscripts and printed books which we discuss or illustrate are listed individually, under 'manuscripts' and 'books' respectively. Titles of works are indexed under the first word except that definite or indefinite articles are ignored, thus *King Alisaunder* and *The King of Tars* may be found under K; *Sir Gawain and the Green Knight* under S; and *Of Arthur and of Merlin* under O. References to figures include information in the figure captions.